# A Different World

Debbie Hodson

———— ∽ ————

IvyStone Press
Emmalena, KY

Published by
IvyStone Press
P.O. Box 50
Emmalena, KY 41740
606/251-3084

Text and Photographs
Copyright © 2014 Debbie Hodson
www.debbiehodson.com

Cover Photographs by Roy Hodson

All rights reserved. No part of this book may be reproduced or transmitted in any form or by any means, electronic or mechanical, including photocopying, recording or by any information storage or retrieval system, without the written permission of the Publisher, except where permitted by law.
For information address: IvyStone Press

ISBN 978-0-9755771-1-0

Printed by Pippa Valley Printing
Emmalena, KY

*To*
*the Stewarts and the Webbs*
*who came and stayed*

# CONTENTS

| | |
|---|---|
| Prologue - A Different World | vii |
| Pieces of the Quilt | 2 |
| Snow Flurries of Summer | 8 |
| That Spot | 12 |
| Ap-pal-a-chi-a | 18 |
| Tastes Like Spring | 24 |
| Sentimental Journey | 32 |
| Like Passin' On Peonies | 38 |
| Appalachian Parade | 42 |
| Delayed Meeting | 48 |
| Just January | 54 |
| Pumping Iron | 58 |
| My Corner of Kentucky | 64 |
| Sleeping Under Love | 68 |
| Up A Creek | 74 |

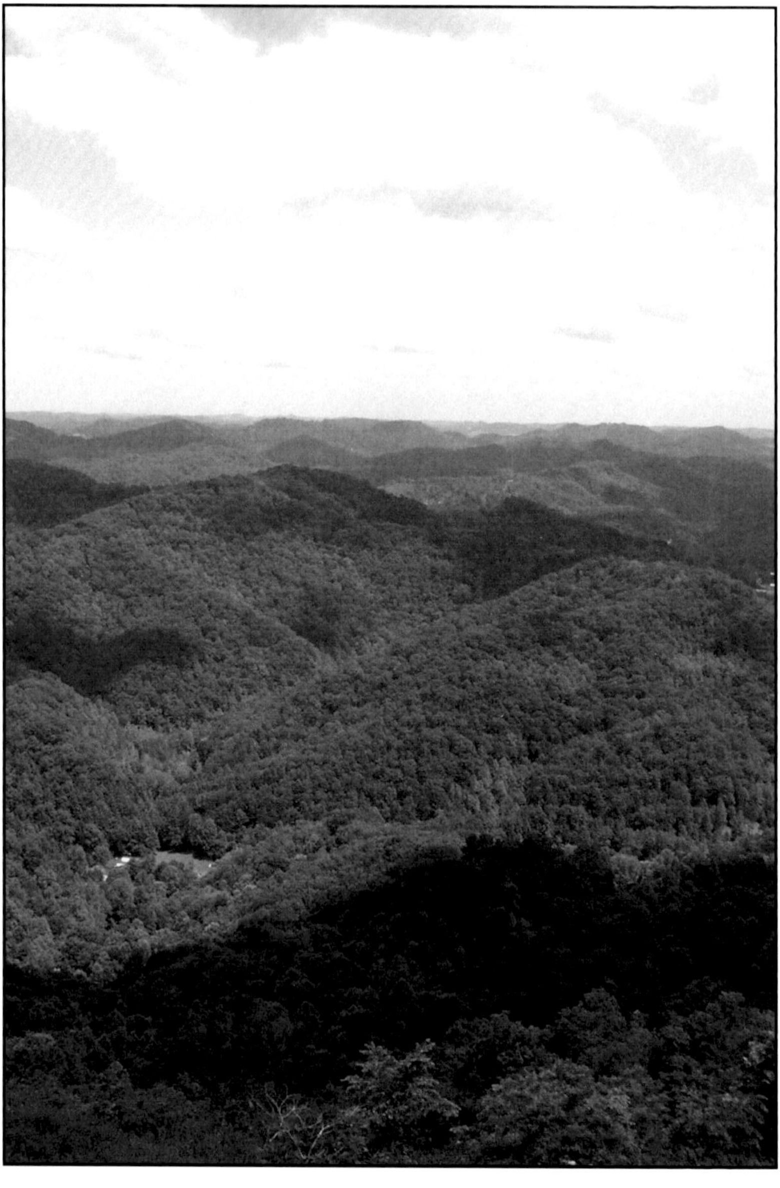

# Prologue
## A Different World

It was one of those events where you have to balance your paper plate and cup and try to eat and talk all at the same time. I'm never good at it. A jigsaw puzzle of serving dishes, all fitted together just so, covered a long buffet table. Cheese balls and crackers, tiny sausages and other bite-sized fare beckoned from plates and platters, ice rattled in glasses and laughter swirled about the room. It was very nice.

A friendly sort of fellow nearby turned to me. "So now, you folks live in Knott County... that's up around Hazard there. I know about where you are. Way back, we'd come that direction to see some of my Dad's family."

I swallowed quickly and smiled. It was good to meet someone with connections to our southeastern part of the state. "Well, that's right near us. We actually live fairly close to Hindman but I can get to

Hazard in just a few minutes, too. We're kind of in-between."

He glanced past me as he spotted someone he knew and waved a hand at them. Somehow, I had the feeling our conversation was about to end.

"Yeah." He paused, tilted his head and seemed to be thinking of something to add. "It sure is a different world up there."

Then he was gone.

*A different world up there.* That could mean the mountains and the hard-to-come-by bottomland in this area make it different from the Bluegrass region or the farm land of western Kentucky. Or that some of the native plants and herbs growing here like yellow root and ginseng aren't as prevalent in other locations. Or it might mean the elk that again roam the ridges of southeastern Kentucky aren't so common elsewhere in the state. It could be things like that.

But I knew the tone of voice. You come to recognize it after a while. Condescending? No, not exactly. Once in a great while, you run into that. But other times, like that day, there's an almost imperceptible nuance, a subtle undertone, that lets you know someone's mindset. They might as well just say there's something so different, so peculiar about this region of Kentucky, it might be best to take it in very small doses. Or maybe not at all.

In a bed and breakfast in another state a while back, I recognized a book on a table of reading material. I knew it featured a collection of photographs of a number of southeastern Kentucky residents. They are critically acclaimed and many find them quite fascinating. Photos of odd, interesting objects, keepsakes, pets, other family members and what-not are captured alongside individuals. Some neglected, run-down dwellings and heartbreaking depictions of poverty appear.

A few faces display smiles caught in lighter moments, but many wear bleak expressions that reveal the quiet resignation often born of hard times, sad situations or difficult circumstances.

I sighed. Maybe I should find a way to look at photographs like that more objectively and learn to appreciate them for their artistic value and the reality of life they capture. Maybe I should be 'bigger' than to let them bother me the way they do. But because I know this part of Kentucky holds so much more than what is often shown, I guess my heart for this region just gets in the way.

Sometimes I wonder, what *do* I want, what is best for this region? Do I want 'outsiders' to only see a place all cleaned up from run-down houses, sad situations and difficult circumstances?

No, I don't want that. The troubling part for me is not that photographs might reflect meager living conditions or instances of poverty. It is the *way* in which people are sometimes photographed that saddens me. And where there are needs and opportunities to help make a difference, human compassion compels us to acknowledge those needs and respond wherever they may be. How wrong it would be to hide them.

What I don't want most of all is for folks who may not have had the advantages in life that some of the rest of us have had, to be photographed in ways that, at least sometimes, seem to provide the likes of a curious sideshow. For the benefit of those 'off from here' who have no balanced context or frame of reference for what this area and its people - the whole big conglomeration of us - are like, I wish every now and then the camera lens could widen enough to reveal the whole picture in southeastern Kentucky.

---

I guess my family would have once fit right in one of those books. My mother and her sisters and brothers were brought up without very much in the way of earthly goods and lived up in a 'holler' near Jenkins. They would have been prime candidates for someone's stark, solemn, black and white photographs. The two older girls in the family married very young, at the ages of fourteen and fifteen, not entirely uncommon in the mountains in the early 1940's. My mother was older, all of sixteen, when she married my father. I can only imagine the expressions a camera might have captured on her face during her childhood years.

Their father sometimes came home drunk, anger spewing like a volcano from what they say was a peaceable, gentle man when sober. Everyone said he was never the same after their son was killed as U.S. troops fought in France during World War II. Maybe he thought someday he could find enough to numb the pain of it all at the bottom of a bottle.

Their mother would take the children up into the woods behind the house to hide out until he simmered down, hunkering behind underbrush, hoping it wouldn't be long. Sometimes, it was awfully cold. Too cold to be the out there, really, but safer out there than in that little frame house perched on the hillside. The grandmother that I only heard about was a good mother, a wonderful mother, I was always told. She loved her children and did what she could for them, gave them the best she had, even if it was only milk and cornbread for supper sometimes.

One night, for some reason, they stayed inside the house. Maybe she didn't see him coming, zigzagging and stumbling up the path from the road. Maybe she and the children had just sat down to eat. Maybe she thought she could settle him down herself and he would finally just collapse and sleep it off.

She was wrong. That night, in a drunken rage, he shot and killed her. Seconds later, he killed himself. My mother and her younger sister, the only two girls still at home, witnessed it all. They were just eleven and nine years old, and those gunshots blew apart their world for a long, long time.

Years later, when I was growing up, it was like my mother closed the door to that period of time in her life. It wasn't that she ever hid it from me, exactly. I knew she would have told me anything I ever asked. Maybe I somehow sensed opening that door just a little crack hurt something inside of her, so I didn't ask her to do it often. When I did, I only caught a glimpse of what I wished I could see.

It was like looking through one of the old timey key holes in the doors in my Papaw's house on Thornton hill. He was my father's mother's father– my great-grandfather– but just Papaw to me. For a time when I was little, we lived in that old house. It had a big side porch where I used to play jacks but the floor boards had bucked up enough in places that it threw the bounce of my ball off and sent it flying in odd directions. There was a well close to the house where Papaw drew up buckets of water. I don't remember much about its interior other than the kitchen. When I try really hard, I can conjure up fragments of the other rooms. Tall windows, wallpaper with some sort of feather-like designs, an old dresser with drawers on either side and a little stool, ceiling lights with strings attached and other random things float through my mind..

But I'll always remember the keyholes. When the big old doors to any upstairs rooms were closed, I was just the right size to squeeze one eye shut and peep through the keyholes. It was interesting to look through those tiny slivers of light. I could perhaps see parts of a bed or dresser, but not the other furniture and objects I knew were in the room. I could try shifting my position or maybe switching eyes, which never worked well, but in the end, I still couldn't see everything I wanted to see. I couldn't see everything I knew had to be there. For a long time, that's how it was with my mother's childhood. There was something more 'in the room' that she wasn't telling me about. Something more that had to be there.

I realize now she was only protecting me, telling me things as she felt I could process them, sparing me from having to comprehend as a young girl myself the tragic circumstance of her parents' deaths and the horror she had had to live through.

One day, when I was about eleven, I told her about a boy on the school bus. He was taller and thin as could be with a face that just looked old, even though he couldn't have been more than a year or so older than I was. His pants were too short, his shoes scuffed and way too big for his feet, his shirts worn thin and frayed. He didn't smell so good. I felt sorry for him. Sometimes, when there was no room elsewhere, he'd stand for a second by my seat and I would scoot over, not altogether eagerly. I didn't mind much, though. He seemed kind of nice. And, it wasn't that long of a ride to school so my endurance was only tested briefly.

I told my mother about him and how the other kids seemed to kind of ignore him and dread when his stop came up. She was peeling potatoes at the kitchen table as I sat there with a glass of chocolate milk in front of me. She put down her knife and looked at me for a minute before she spoke. I could tell it was going to be something serious. Her eyes told me I had better pay attention. Then she spoke very softly. "I don't want you to ever, ever make fun of someone or look down on them because they have less than you do. Never, ever. Do you hear me?"

I saw a hint of tears in her eyes and I promised, with all my heart, I would never, ever, do that. The next day when the boy got on the bus, I scooted over right away. I don't think he stood there a second.

As I grew older and the slivers of light in the keyholes enlarged enough for me to see things clearly, I realized my mother knew the painful stigma of growing up without much and feeling insecure and inferior because of it. After the awfulness of her parents' deaths, she knew what it was like for her family to be the whispered topic of conversation among her classmates and in the community, at least for a while. She knew what it was like to be robbed of something precious at a very young age. Later, as a grown woman with children of her own, she couldn't right all the wrongs in this world but she could make sure her daughter never, ever measured someone just by their background or the amount of their possessions.

There are still sad situations and difficult circumstances to be found up in the 'hollers' here. Some of people's own making, some not. There are folks living in tiny shacks, getting by on next to nothing. There are children who have scarcely been outside the county they were born in, who have never been in an elevator, never had a vacation or hardly anything of what many kids today call 'normal.'

There are girls who get pregnant and drop out of school, boys who figure they can get by and don't need any more education or training. And there are plenty, young and old, whose lives have been ruined by drug abuse. But that's not all there is to this place. Or any other place, actually.

---

My heart sank when I saw someone looking at that book at the B&B the next day. From my seat nearby, I could tell that, at least in that particular book, the almost bizarre expressions on some of the subject's faces were sort of startling to the gentleman. I let it go for a while, watching his own facial expressions of frowns, widened eyes, pursed lips, a raised eyebrow or two and quizzical looks.

Finally, when I could stand it no longer, I spoke up and told him I lived in the very area displayed in its pages. "Is this accurate, then?" he wanted to know. I told him that, yes, those who were photographed in the book he held were just as real and part of the culture here as I am.

But I also explained how disheartening it is to see the way this part of Kentucky is often portrayed, and shared with him, from my over fifty years experience, what I believe is a better, more complete understanding of the region. He closed the book and listened respectfully. A small victory. But what if I hadn't been there?

*A different world up there.* Thank goodness. It's our world. It belongs to those of us who have roots that go way down, deep in these mountains and to those of us that have been wrapped up and cradled for years in the valleys and 'hollers' that lie between them. We like their 'claustrophobic' shelter and the break from cold, harsh winds they offer. We value the serenity and security they bring to our minds in the busyness and craziness of life.

This world belongs to those who love its beauty and know the rhythm and rhyme each season brings to it just as well as we know our names. The culture and tradition, the music, the plants and wildflowers, the wildlife, from tiny salamanders along the creeks to the massive elk up in the mountains – all of it is ours. It nourishes our spirits. It makes us who we are. It's a different world. And it's a *good* world.

Those of us born in the 'baby boomer' years between 1946 to 1963 have witnessed so many changes in Kentucky's Appalachia. I like to think we have a pretty good vantage point. We are fortunate enough to have personally known many old-timers of previous generations who lived close to the land, raised big gardens 'by the signs,' kept chickens and at least a milk cow, slaughtered hogs on cold November days, simmered big kettles of apple butter, strung up shucky beans every summer and raised children on goodly portions of soup beans and cornbread.

We've seen roads laden with coal trucks making haul after haul in boom years and listened to the sad silence of the trains and trucks when coal was 'down.' We've lived long enough to remember the bustling downtowns of Whitesburg, Fleming-Neon,

Hindman, Hazard, Harlan, filled with so many people you couldn't stir 'em with a stick, people shopping at hardware stores, dime stores and ordering grilled cheese and Cokes at counters of drugstores.

We've watched store-lined main streets morph into avenues of attorney offices and insurance agencies as development left downtowns. We've seen the advent of fast food restaurants, four-lane highways, expansions in educational opportunities, construction of shopping centers, medical centers, growth in business and options for entertainment.

It seems our generation is the bridge between the old and new, between the Appalachia in our memories and the Appalachia in our future. A lot of people are wondering, what is our future going to be like now? The coal we thought would almost last forever or as far into forever as we could see, is done, they say. We're listening to the sad silence of the trains and trucks once again and many pronounce this time it's different, this time that silence is going to last.

Maybe so. Time will tell. The trail ahead might not be easy. It might mean exploring new territory and new ways of doing things. The uncertainty of it all might make us uncomfortable, perhaps even fearful, if we are honest. It might take grit and determination. But we will find a way. We will *make* a way. That's what mountain people do.

As together, our hands and the younger hands of those coming behind us grasp all the future holds for this region of Kentucky, let's be sure to hold on tight to the things in our Appalachian culture that have enriched our lives, shaped us and made us the kind of people we are today. If we do that, I can't help but believe the future here will be very, very bright.

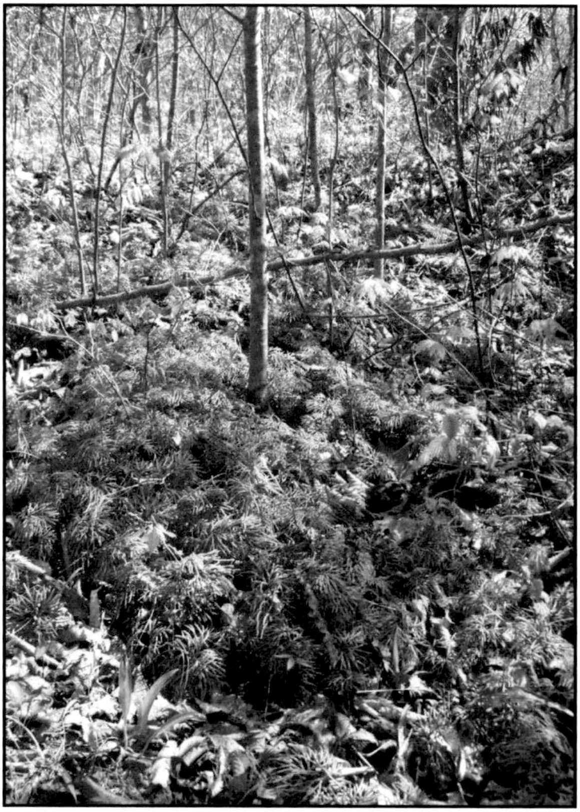

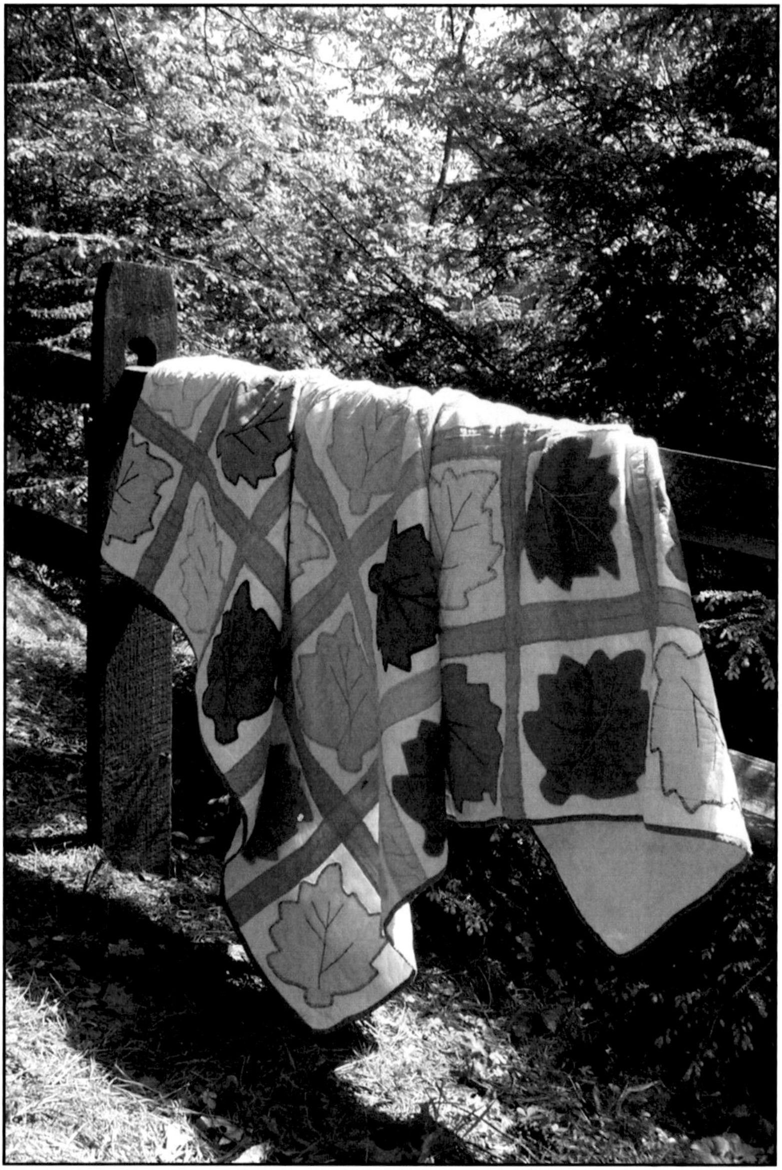

## *Pieces of the Quilt*

There's something special about families in my part of Appalachia. I guess it has to do with the connections that families provide. Those cords of kin connect us to the stream of early settlers that challenged this land long ago and join us, as well, to those who will come after us. It's a good feeling, this Appalachian family connection.

They were hardy souls who opened up the mountains back then and stayed for the long haul because they loved them, with whatever flaws or obstacles they presented, for better or worse, for richer or poorer. They had to be cut from a different cloth and blessed with a dose of plain old hardheadedness just to settle here and make a go of it. Others moved through and headed west looking for the rich, fertile soil and good farm land they'd heard about. Still others retreated back east. But some stayed and we're part of that clan.

Unlike people who live in heavily populated cities, those of us here in the hills usually know the folks around us. By and large, we're not a transient lot. We know our neighbors because we likely know their families - their parents, grandparents, aunts and uncles, even cousins. And that's a heap of knowing.

I realize there are other areas of the country that are equally rural and share many of these same qualities, but it is especially true of our southern mountain culture. We're part of a generational 'quilt' of mountain people, pieced together over time, a rich, colorful display of different families and ancestors, yet stitched and bound with the common thread of our Appalachian heritage. We are placed by our families, what county they are from and what ever-so-tiny community within that county. For us, it's a source of identity, a sense of belonging and of fitting into the puzzle somewhere. I like that.

Once, on a blistering early September day, I stood in the crowd at our local fall Gingerbread festival. Folks bunched up along the sidewalks waiting for the annual parade and, to pass the time, I started a conversation with the older couple standing beside me. Turns out, they were from the adjoining county and had decided to come over for the day to enjoy the parade and displays of crafts. That got my curiosity up since that county was where I had lived during some of my growing up years.

I asked what part of the county they lived in and was kind of surprised to learn they were from the same small community as my family. I ought to be able to place them, I thought, even though it had been a long time since I had moved away from home. After I studied their faces a little more and made adjustments for what over twenty years had done to them and me, I remembered them as customers in my grandmother's little country restaurant. I had probably even waited on them when I helped out sometimes as a teenager.

"So, you're Fernoy and Shirley's girl!" the gentleman exclaimed. "Now, that means Sadie was your grandmother. Well, well, how about that?" As the parade got underway, our conversation was interrupted but afterwards we talked a bit more, recalling a few mutual acquaintances that lived roundabout that little community. Then we said goodbye.

On the way home, I thought about that chance meeting. Those folks hadn't known me by sight, at least not at first, seeing as how I had married and moved off to other parts of southeastern Kentucky years before. And I hadn't recognized them right away, either. As we talked, though, that old familiar connection of kin and communities brought us close together again, if only for a few minutes. Yes, I am Shirley's girl. And Sadie's granddaughter. I'm pieced in, part of the quilt, a little twig on the branch of the mountain women in my family tree.

My encounter with that couple reminds me of a story told about a Hollywood actor and director who came to this area of Kentucky a number of years ago to make a movie. The actor, well known for his action films and expertise in martial arts, stopped one day by the roadside where an older local gentleman had 'set up shop' selling his handmade wooden crafts.

As he talked with the craftsman, it became apparent the old fellow had no idea his customer was a film star of considerable fame. A little perplexed, the Hollywood actor asked, "You don't know who I am, do you?"

After pondering on that a few seconds, the mountain entrepreneur replied, "No, I reckon I don't. Whose boy are you?"

I smile every time I think about that because it's such a perfect illustration of how we know each other, what our reference points are - families, kin and communities. Yes, those of us from Kentucky's Appalachia are connected. And, in a way that's hard to explain, we are also connected, pieced together, if you will, by the shared, deep love for this region that is practically stamped right on us at birth.

Our mountain heritage, with all its tradition, wisdom and 'connections,' is handed down to us by our kinfolks like a cherished old platter or well-worn pocket watch. It is the common bond that encircles us, holds us together and gives us the long lasting, deep-seated pride of place that we value so much.

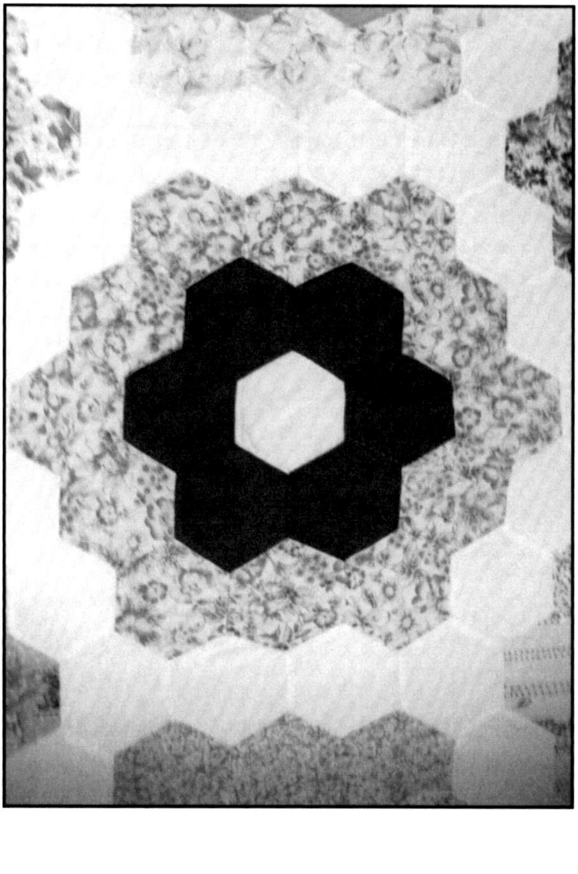

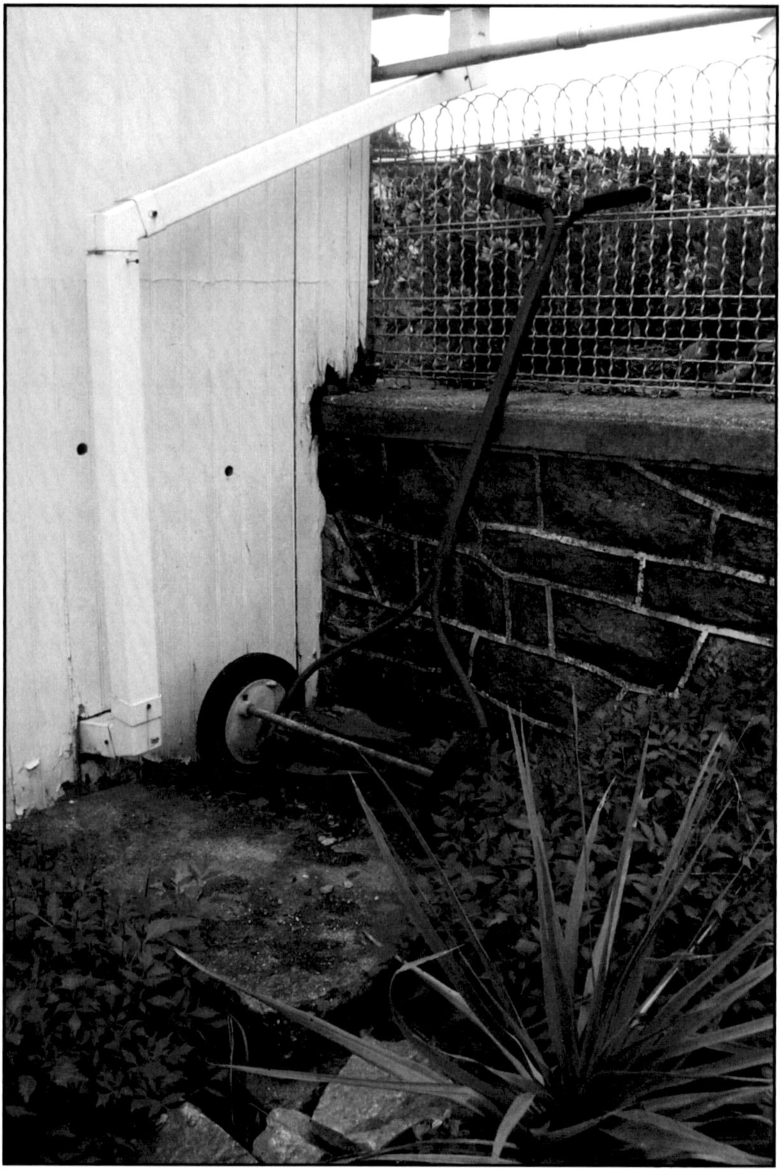

# *Snow Flurries of Summer*

I wasn't even sure they made them anymore, but right there in the magazine was a picture to prove it, along with an ad for old-fashioned push mowers. According to the magazine article, one can still be purchased for anywhere up to three hundred dollars, and three hundred dollars ought to surely buy a 'Cadillac' of reel mowers.

It's funny how early memories usually sleep in cobwebbed corners of our minds, waking when triggered by something in the present that carries us to the past. A book, a song, a scent or just the mention of a name can send us on a journey that places us, temporarily, in another time and place. That magazine picture of two reel mowers resting against a tree carried me back to my grandmother's house up on a hill in Letcher County and evenings spent listening to the whir and click of my great-grandfather's old push mower.

While growing up, I loved to watch him mow the

lawn as the mower's blades manicured the side yard nigh unto putting green perfection, had there not been a decided slope on the north end. Occasionally, he would push just a little too far into the hydrangea bush that graced the side of the house, scattering snow flurries of white petals across the smooth, green grass.

Papaw took meticulous care of his mower, which, as I recall, required no elaborate maintenance other than the oil he squirted on it from a small, skinny-spouted can. He would be sure to clean off any clumps of damp grass clinging to the blades before storing it in the shed by the smokehouse.

Where the yard ended, he turned to his scythe, and toiled away with a methodical 'whoosh,' cutting the tall weeds, pausing to push his hat back from his brow and lean against the handle now and then. Sweat darkened the band of his hat and wet the back of his shirt. Seeing him standing there now, in my mind's eye, makes me think of other things.

We often toured the outbuildings together - the smokehouse, the barn, the hen house to gather eggs. We picked up June apples and sniffed the heady aroma of drooping peonies. He often let me help draw water from the well. The old well bucket plunged down, down into the far-away darkness and then, in a matter of seconds, began its return voyage. Closer and closer it came until it arrived brimming full of cold, clear water. We drank it, in all its thirst-quenching sweetness, from the incredibly light, hollowed-out gourd Papaw kept nearby.

Buckets of memories spill over now. He was a mountain man but not exactly a mountain of a man, at least not in physical frame. By then, he was a little hunched with age but still dapper in sharply creased trousers, suspenders, long-sleeved shirt and hat.

As a former railroad employee, he treated time with respect. No guesswork. When asked the time, he would draw out his gold pocket watch tethered on its chain, observe the bold face, the sweep of the second hand, and declare precisely the time - "2:37 PM." He measured his words in the same careful manner, thinking before he spoke, conscious of how he phrased things, earnest in giving the best answer to a question.

Our treks together to the tiny post office in our community were often taken in near silence but, nevertheless, I learned from him as I watched him interact with the postmaster, the owner of the country store nearby and the assembly of gentlemen often found whittling away as they sat on the store's front porch.

As the years passed, he taught me about weather signs like rings around the moon and 'mare's tails' in the sky. What Papaw couldn't tell about the weather from outward signs, he told from a surprisingly accurate inward one - his rheumatism. "Rain's a-movin' in tomorrow. I can feel it in my legs," he would predict. He ate oatmeal every morning, even if accompanied by eggs or biscuits and gravy. Evidently, he was privy to something long before modern-day nutritionists extolled the virtues of oats.

I missed him terribly when he died. Now I listen as our grass is cut to the drone of a riding mower and the buzz of a string trimmer. The world is different; life goes on. Still, I wish my sons could have heard the whir and click of that old mower's wheels and blades on a June mountain evening and known the man who was their great-great grandfather. Maybe I'll take a look at that ad for reel mowers again. Perhaps we could use one, at least over in the side yard. It's too bad we don't have a big hydrangea bush, though.

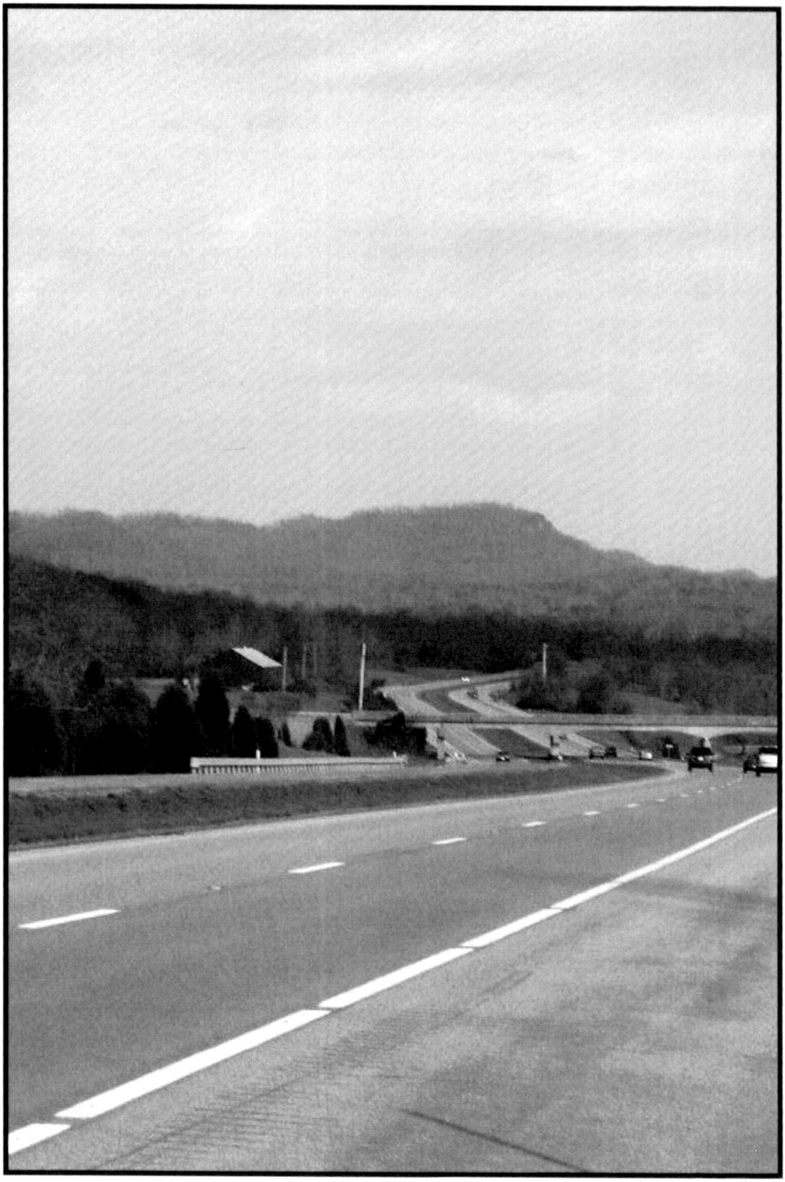

## That Spot

We picked up a friend from out of state at the airport in Lexington and headed home. As we navigated past shopping centers and housing developments and then back onto the interstate, we were eager to catch up on things in her life and hear about another trip she had taken to Austria and Switzerland. Enthusiastic and full of smiles, she was more well-travelled in her young life than I'd likely ever be.

She recounted her adventures and answered our questions as we drove along. I was relieved. It had been a long day and the conversation made the next couple of hours go by more quickly than usual. As we made our way closer to home and the scenery of the gentle Appalachian mountains of Kentucky surrounded us, our friend reflected quietly, "Wow. It's so pretty around here."

"Yes," I agreed, surveying the evening shadows

just beginning to fall across the mountains. "It is. It truly is."

Unlike our well-travelled friend, I've never had opportunity to see the mountains of Austria or Switzerland, unless you count what I've seen in *National Geographic Magazine* or in *The Sound of Music*. My experience with mountains of any kind was pretty much limited to those of the mid and southern Appalachians until we once drove out west on a family vacation.

In the weeks prior to our trip, we accumulated a library of brochures and magazine articles. We sought out and talked with others who had been to Colorado and Wyoming. They shared lodging tips with us and some carried on about the fact that we were going to get to see what 'real' mountains looked like. Needless to say, we were quite excited about the upcoming trip.

Several days into our journey that summer, as we neared our first destination in Wyoming, the snow-capped peaks of the Grand Tetons rose out of the horizon, jutting into the skyline with a thundering presence. They stood proudly with rugged, faceted slopes that led to deep ravines and canyons. My hands couldn't find the camera fast enough. They were mountains, all right.

Later in the week, in Colorado, the Rockies awaited with equally beautiful scenery. There were meadows of wildflowers and, even in August, snow lingered on the tops of many mountains. The views were spectacular and breathtaking. I'd seen calendar pages with scenes like that but never witnessed them with my own eyes.

Two weeks and many photos later, we found ourselves on the trip home, driving east from Colorado through the amazingly flat countryside of Kansas. We eventually plodded into Missouri, then on into Illinois and Indiana. Finally, after many weary hours, we crossed back over the state line of Kentucky.

Even after those tiring miles, some more time in the car lay ahead in order to really get back home, back to our house tucked far in the mountains of southeastern Kentucky. Early the next morning we pressed on, anxious to arrive before too late in the day.

As we drove the last leg of our journey, the landscape changed once again as, gradually, the rolling hills of central Kentucky's Bluegrass region became more pronounced and drew closer together. In a while, up ahead in the distance, like an old worn and comfortable flannel shirt, the first hints of the Appalachian Mountains I knew and loved appeared. I'd been waiting for that spot.

It was a familiar stretch in the road and a place many from this part of Kentucky know well. When we go gallivanting off to far away places around the globe, to the land of 'Up North' across the Ohio or maybe just to Lexington, it's the view seen on the Bert Combs Mountain Parkway near Clay City that gives our hearts a little leap. It's the spot where, driving home from acres of farms and fields, from big cities and suburbs, we first glimpse the mountains we know so well, the ones we've seen rise out of the morning fog a thousand times. And you just can't help but smile.

As we turned a few more curves that day, the mountains were soon no longer distant on the horizon but close up, all around us. I examined them with new eyes. Lush with late summer leaves turning in the breeze, they were serene and beautiful with a quiet dignity all their own. Not striking and bold, commanding my attention, but subtly seeking it with their regal manner, drawing me in with their beauty, welcoming me home.

Just as some folks had predicted, we had seen some 'real' mountains on our trip out west, some awe-inspiring and beautiful ones. But I also acknowledged, as I took in the scene before me, those old time-worn southeastern Kentucky mountains looked awfully beautiful to me. My little corner of the blanket of the great Appalachians would do just fine and I sure was glad to be wrapped back up in it again.

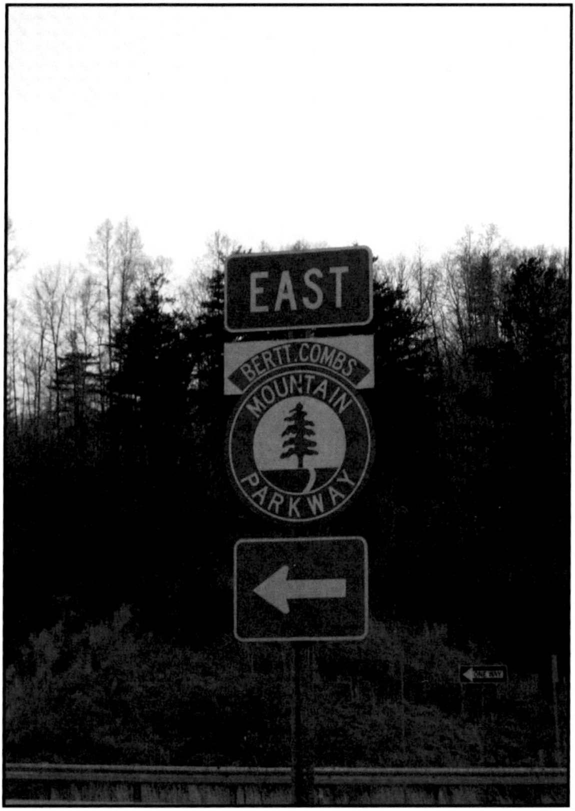
EAST
BERT T. COMBS
MOUNTAIN
PARKWAY
ONE WAY

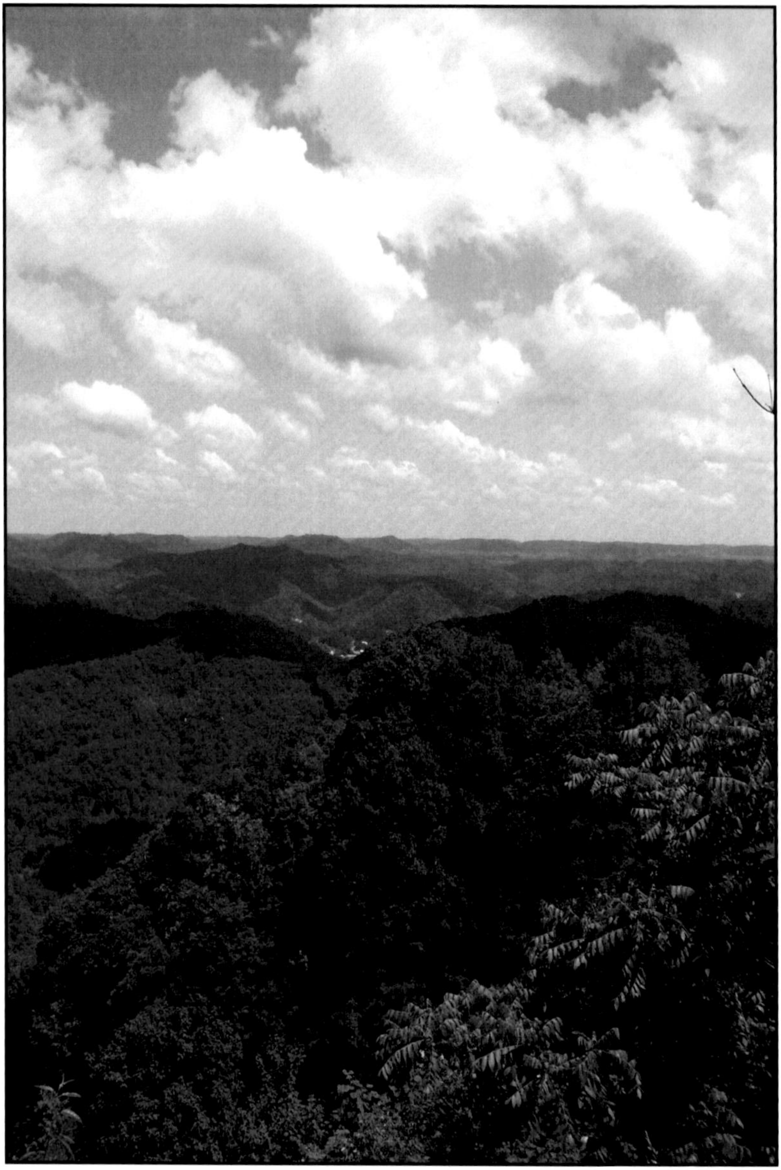

## Ap-pa-la-chi-a

    Appalachia. I've always liked saying that word. I like the way it sort of tumbles off my tongue in a cascade of syllables. Ap-pa-la-chi-a. That word holds a host of images for me.
    I can see the mountains rising and falling into the horizon, their myriad shades of green covering every contour with a beauty that, sometimes, takes my breath away. I can picture the warm glow of the mountains on October days, days bright with a palette of orange, red and gold and strung together with nothing but crisp air, sunshine and blue sky.
    I can see the moon on a clear December night, suspended high above the outline of Pine Mountain like a single, perfect pearl. But should all those images someday fade from my mind, I hope one will remain - that of the redbud trees in spring. The color

of those redbud blossoms, kind of like someone swirled buckets of pink and purple paint into one marvelous mix and splashed it all over the mountainsides, is nothing short of wonderful.

Looking back, I realize I was about fifteen years old before I learned there were other images attached to the word 'Appalachia'. Before I knew some people, in some places, considered those from this region to be backward and ignorant, lazy and shiftless. Inferior, somehow. Just hillbillies.

"I'm not from *that* part of Kentucky," I heard Emily say with special emphasis on the "that", as I walked away from the group of girls one summer day long ago. She added in a low but still audible voice, "That's where the hillbillies live." I felt the sting of her words and the stab into a soft, tender part of me that, until that day, I hardly knew was there.

Emily was from Kentucky, but not from my part of Kentucky. She lived much further to the west in the part of the state where long, level fields of corn and tobacco grew in abundance. In that social gathering, she wanted to assure the other teenaged girls she was far removed from the area of my heritage in southeastern Kentucky's Appalachian region. And, more importantly, far removed from the so-called "hillbillies" that lived there.

I cringed inside and didn't let on I had heard as I focused on the sidewalk in front of me. Still in the throes of a case of shyness that almost incapacitated me early on, I couldn't muster the courage needed to confront her. Surely, I remember thinking, every place probably had a few undesirable characters. Maybe not hillbillies but ...*something*. And while, perhaps, there were some people here in the mountains who might fit the descriptions of backward and ignorant, lazy and shiftless, I didn't know too many.

I knew intelligent, hard-working people. Storekeepers and coal miners. Nurses. Teachers. Waitresses and carpenters. Truck drivers. Secretaries. Salesmen. Bank tellers. Friendly, decent people who raised gardens, went to church, helped their neighbors and taught their children to be respectful and honest.

I tried to imagine why Emily felt the way she did about the area where I was from. Deep inside, though, I knew. I knew the battlegrounds of President Lyndon Johnson's war on poverty were located more or less in my backyard. I knew there were families in Appalachia living in real need. I knew there were people isolated in nooks and crannies of the mountains who had a hard time reaching places that could provide the education they needed. I knew receiving adequate health care posed a real problem for some folks. I was young, but I saw the problems in my part of Appalachia.

I had also observed enough, though, to realize lack did not always mean laziness and little opportunity did not necessarily parallel little intelligence. Even families I knew that didn't have much, kept their small, simple homes tidy, welcomed opportunities for themselves and their children to learn and respected themselves and their community.

I saw creativity and ingenuity and intelligence everywhere I looked. I saw it in those who could look at the sky and predict the next day's weather and who planted gardens 'by the signs' with almost geometric precision. I saw it in the painstaking attention to detail and design among those who hand-stitched beautiful quilts or made baskets. I noticed it in uniform strings of beans hanging from porches and shelves bowing under jewel-toned jars of canned vegetables and fruit. I observed it in men and women who butchered hogs with matter-of-fact, surgical-like deftness on chilly fall days.

I heard it in the words of those who knew the mountains like the backs of their hands, who could identify every tree and wildflower and tell how to use the herbs that grew in the rich, loamy soil. I heard it through the hands of those who filled the air with music from fiddles, guitars and banjos.

And, yes, I witnessed it in the lives of those who read and studied, went on to college and did whatever was necessary in order to become teachers, doctors, attorneys, business people and other professionals engaged in a wide variety of careers.

Regardless of the opinion some had of the area and the prevalent references to hillbillies, I knew the whole story, not just parts of it, and I was proud of the background I had in the mountains of Appalachia.

Today, I've seen enough of this country to know most places do have some undesirable characters and, unfortunately, a number of people who are needy and struggling with poverty. In upscale suburbs as well as one-horse towns there are unmotivated and irresponsible individuals. No area can lay claim to all of them. I suspect it's always been that way.

To be fair, I admit I've had preconceived notions about other people and places 'off from here.' There was a time I assumed folks in urban areas were unfriendly and rude and people from up North were kind of snooty and uppity. And more than once, I've entertained the idea that a good portion of the population of California is rather eccentric. It seems carrying around those kinds of assumptions is an easy thing for some of us to do and it takes conscious effort not to make hasty, unfair judgments.

The hurtful words I overheard that summer day so long ago are nothing but a faint, faint, echo now. I know what I've always known. I am proud to be from southeastern Kentucky, proud to say I have a claim to this place, to know many years ago my kinfolk stayed and made a life for themselves here in these mountains.

Appalachia. I like saying that word just as much as ever. And, most of all, I like the feeling that comes from knowing "*that* part of Kentucky", that *Appalachian* part of Kentucky, is the place I call home.

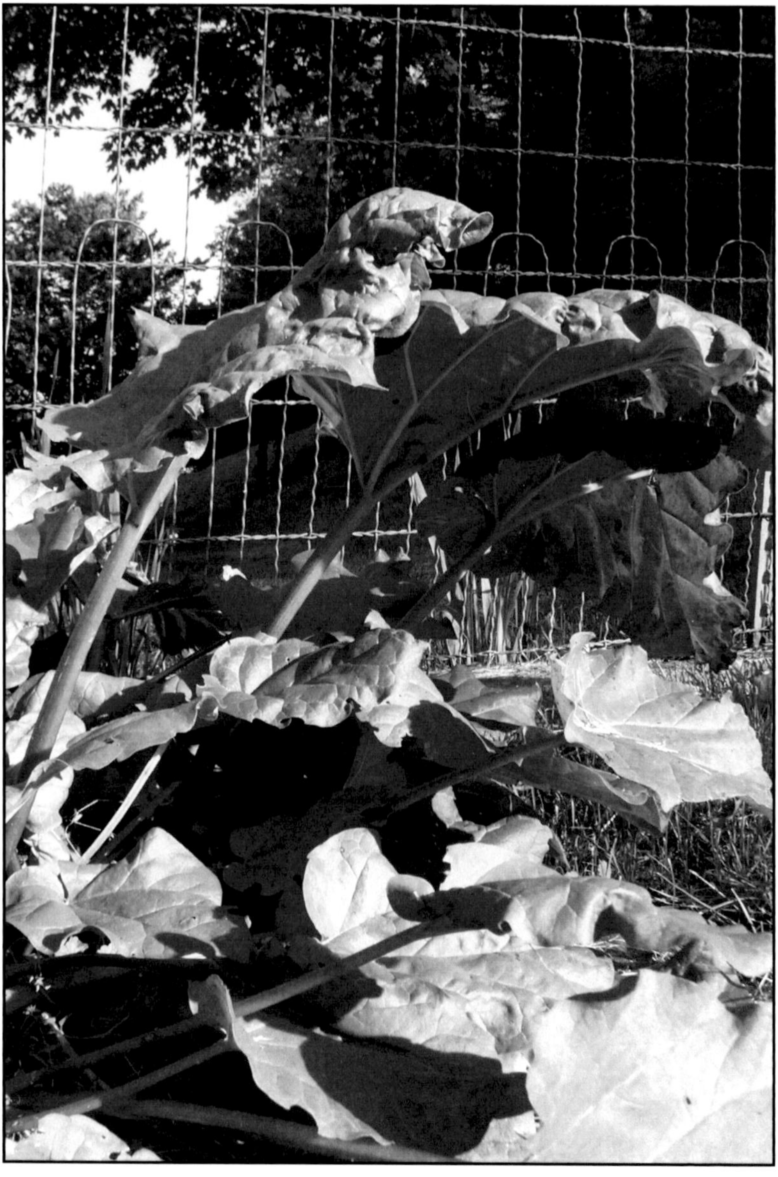

## Tastes Like Spring

"Eat a mess of 'poke' in the spring and you won't have to see the doctor all year." At least, that's what I've heard some old-timers around here say. Granny didn't say that in so many words, but she did cook up a few messes of poke sallet (not to be confused with *salad* - that's a whole different thing) every spring. Maybe she believed it was some kind of tonic. I liked those cooked greens ('sallet' is an Old English word for a mess of young greens and I'm sure you know what a 'mess' is), but there wasn't much Granny cooked that I didn't like. It was a sure sign of spring when she took a notion to go looking for some 'poke.'

That old 'poke' fed a lot of mountaineers back in the day. It was a welcome sight when those tender little shoots started coming out of the ground. It meant something fresh and green to cook when 'put up' food supplies ran low after a hard winter. It meant a little more food on the table when there was a bunch of hungry young-un's to feed. Poke, nettle leaves and other edible greens were often served in spring. As we know now, those plants provide calcium and other needed minerals so those women were giving their families a boost in nutrition as well as filling bellies. A few 'messes of poke' likely kept a lot of them from needing a doctor.

Another sign of spring was when Papaw was out in the garden tending to the peas he faithfully planted every Valentine's Day. *Every* Valentine's Day, no matter the bone-chilling cold or flurries of snow. I never questioned the reason behind his timing. I just figured planting peas on Valentine's Day was something everyone did like going to church Easter Sunday or having a picnic on the Fourth of July. For all I knew, the peas wouldn't grow right or taste right if you planted them any other day.

Later on, we reaped the benefits of Papaw's faithfulness to the task as we relished the taste of those fresh garden peas for Sunday dinners. Granny would use her good dishes, ones I later learned were bought from traveling salesmen that peddled their wares through the mountains. At the time, I thought those plates, with their colorful splashes of hand-painted flowers, were really fine china. With ham and cornbread and deviled eggs and mashed potatoes, those peas tasted like spring to me and couldn't have tasted better if they *had* been served on the finest china.

Poke sallet, garden peas, as well as green onions, new potatoes, fresh-picked lettuce and strawberries right from the patch, all provide tastes of spring. My mother's homemade strawberry shortcake ranks a very close second, but the dish I most associate with spring has to be rhubarb cobbler. Papaw's rhubarb stood close to the smokehouse, right along the path that led out to the hen house. On his way to gather eggs, he kept an eye on it, brushing the broad leaves aside to check its progress. When the stalks were big and fat and tall (and he had sampled some), he'd pronounce it ready.

That's when Granny got out mixing bowls and made rhubarb pies and cobblers. To this day, I just can't officially celebrate spring until I make at least one of those myself. And though I know strawberries with rhubarb can be complimentary, I'd rather use rhubarb alone and just enough sugar so that it still kind of sets your teeth on edge.

For a long time, I just assumed everyone liked rhubarb. I learned otherwise one spring when I served some guests a fresh rhubarb pie, warm from the oven in a deep-dish pie plate. When I made it that day, I had even thrown in an extra scoop or two of sugar, bearing in mind our company might have more of a taste for sweetness than I did. As a further measure of safety, I also had ice cream on hand.

When I placed the pie on the table and announced what kind it was, I could tell they seemed less than enthusiastic. Being good friends, they confessed their dislike of rhubarb and I appreciated their honesty. Ice cream to the rescue.

Oh, well. I learned something - not everyone likes rhubarb. I suppose everyone doesn't like poke sallet, either. And, who knows, there are probably a few 'quare' folks out there who don't even like fresh garden peas. It's such a shame. How can folks like that ever really get a good taste of spring?

## Sadie's Rhubarb Cobbler

5 cups rhubarb
cut into one inch pieces
1 cup sugar (can use 3/4 cup if tartness is desired)
2 tablespoons of cornstarch
2 tablespoons real butter
1/3 cup of water
1/4 teaspoon cinnamon
1/8 teaspoon nutmeg

Place all above in medium size kettle. Bring to boil, starting on low heat. Stir often so it doesn't scorch. Turn heat higher slowly as you monitor and stir. When it begins to boil, turn down and keep stirring and cooking for a few minutes till thickens and becomes slightly juicy. Pour filling into 8" baking dish.

**To make topper:**
1 cup all purpose flour
3 tablespoons sugar
1 and 1/2 teaspoons baking powder
1/4 teaspoon salt
1/4 cup real butter, room temperature
1/4 cup milk
1 large beaten egg
1 teaspoon vanilla

Mix all dry ingredients in bowl. Cut in butter with pastry blender till fine and crumbly. Combine milk, egg and vanilla. Add to dry ingredients and mix well. Add a little more milk if needed to moisten the dry mixture. Place small mounds of dough on top of filling. Bake at 400 degrees for 20 minutes, turn down to 350, bake 5 more min. Cool to warm and serve with whipped cream or ice cream.

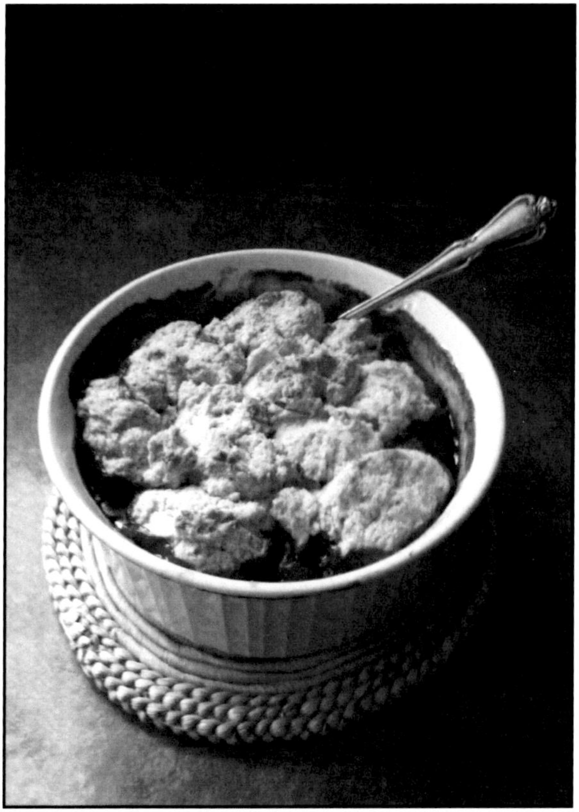

## Shirley's Shortcake

2 cups all purpose flour
1 and 1/2 teaspoons baking powder
1/2 teaspoon salt
3/4 cup sugar
2 and 1/2 tablespoon soft, room temperature butter
2 and 1/2 tablespoons solid shortening such as Crisco
2/3 cup milk
1 teaspoon vanilla (or almond flavoring)

Place dry ingredients in mixing bowl, stir lightly to mix well. With pastry blender, cut in butter and shortening, to resemble fine crumbs.

Combine milk and vanilla in separate bowl. Add all at once to dry ingredients. Using a fork, stir and mix together.

If some of the dry ingredients are not moistened, add milk a little at a time until dough clings together and leaves the sides of the bowl.

With spatula, scrape mixture into a greased 8 or 9 inch cake pan, smooth top evenly to edges. Bake at 425 degrees till tests done.

## Strawberries for Cake

Wash well and remove stems and leaves from one or more quarts of strawberries. Slice berries into pieces and place in large bowl. Add one cup of sugar and stir gently. (For more than one quart of berries, of course, you will need additional sugar. Adjust to taste, depending on the sweetness you prefer) Allow the bowl to stand at room temperature while the sugar and berry combination forms juice as the sugar dissolves.

## To Serve

Cut warm cake into individual serving pieces. Place on plates. Carefully slice each piece into 2 layers. Spoon strawberries over the bottom piece. Cover with remaining layer and spoon more berries over the top piece of cake. Place a scoop of whipped cream on the very top and serve.

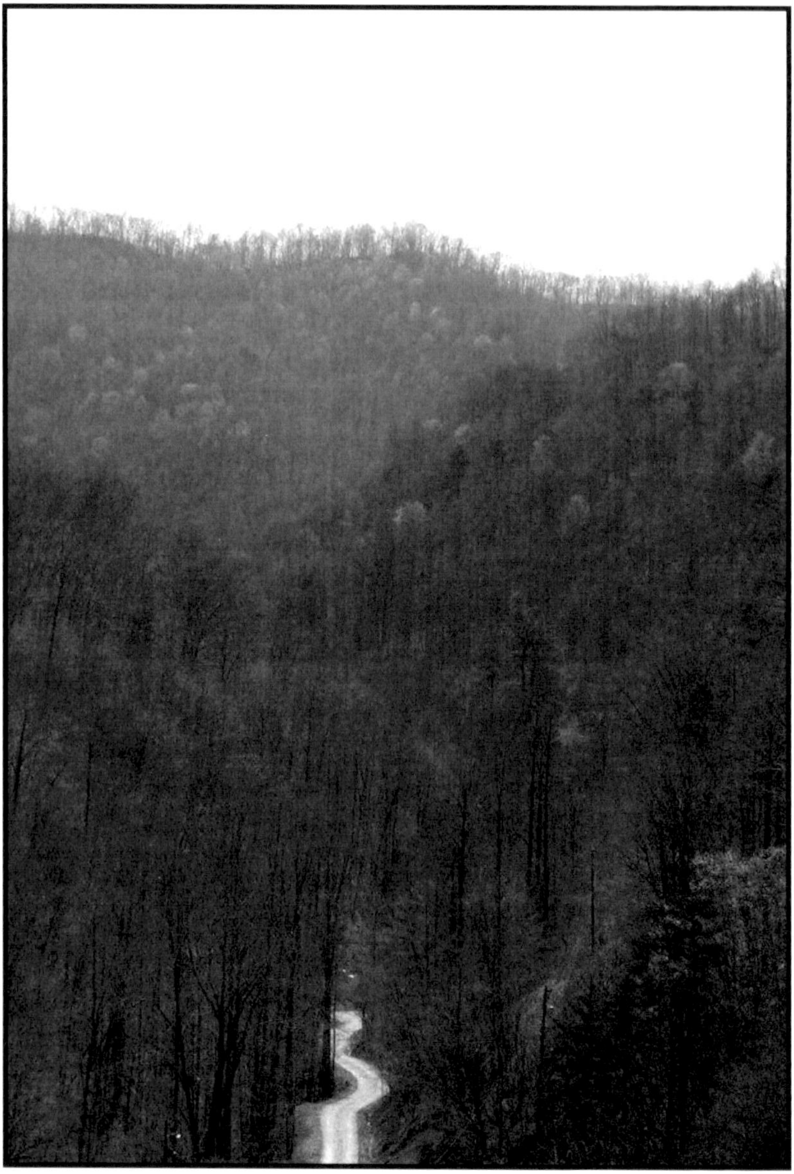

## *Sentimental Journey*

Sometimes out of state visitors to our region tell me it doesn't look like very many people live around here. I want to reply, "What? You've got to be kidding. There are lots of people living around here." But since I realize their question really stems from a lack of knowledge, I can't fault them too much.

Instead, I explain that by traveling into the area as they did, on some of the highways built most recently, they simply weren't able to see where a good portion of the population lives. When crisscrossing the region on the older two-lane roads though, weaving through the mountains and meandering along the creeks, it's much easier to glimpse the small towns, side roads and hollows that give evidence that there are, indeed, quite a few people living around here.

Of course, I don't drive on those old roads much either these days, but sometimes I sort of miss them.

Don't get me wrong. I don't miss the torturous little journey we used to make when I was young from our area of southeastern Kentucky over into the mountains of southwest Virginia to visit relatives. Or the curving, winding roads that took us to bigger towns for events like buying school clothes or seeing 'the specialist' or Christmas shopping. We poked along behind one slow-moving coal truck after another, until by some stroke of good fortune, a 'straight stretch' appeared.

Recently, however, I decided to reacquaint myself with some of those old roads. One Saturday, my husband and I drove into Letcher County, back to where I lived during some of my childhood years. We exited from the big four-lane highway off onto the more narrow roads we used long ago. Though a lot of things had changed, I was surprised at what I could see through memories resurrected just by traveling those roads again.

There's a school now standing near the field where they used to set up the open-air roller rink in the summer. On warm nights it attracted quite a crowd. Often I was in that crowd, lacing up clunky white (well, sort of white) skates that had obviously been laced many times by others before me. The juke box blared popular tunes and couples anticipated the 'slow skate' numbers. Sadly, just when my sweaty hands got brave enough to release the rail for a minute or two, it would be time for the rink to come down.

In several of the towns and communities that I knew so well, many buildings and landmarks were still there, in their same old places. The building that housed my dentist's office, others that once were drugstores, hardware stores, clothing stores, dime stores, were all accounted for, though perhaps serving other purposes in more recent times. How funny it was to suddenly see myself perched on a drugstore stool drinking a chocolate soda or root beer float, scrounging in my pockets for change to buy a pack of gum at the dime store, walking down the street with friends, shopping with my mother for an Easter dress or school shoes.

We passed houses where friends and acquaintances of my parents had once lived. Names and faces I hadn't thought of in years came back to me. People long forgotten and some no longer living, appeared in my mind. I could see them on their porches stringing beans and hanging them up to dry, hoeing in their gardens, putting wash on the line, throwing hands up to wave at those passing by.

One by one the old familiar coal towns with post offices, commissaries and uniformly constructed houses, some tidy and cared for, others in sad disrepair, sailed past the car window. Then the remnants of the old drive-in theater appeared, still visible among weeds and bramble. I recalled summer nights with cheeseburgers and milkshakes perched on trays attached to the car window as John Wayne's voice crackled through the speaker and his image loomed on the big screen.

We turned up into the hollow where some relatives had lived. Smooth, black pavement replaced the rough road that had formerly served residents of the hollow. And yes, there was the spot where Dock Franklin's store once catered to the needs of that community. Nowadays, big super centers with merchandise piled to the ceilings, have nothing on Dock.

As a child, I was fascinated by the fact that, from a single vantage point, one could lay eyes on anything and everything one might need in life. Or so it seemed. At that point, though, about all I ever needed were Popsicles and chocolate-covered ice cream bars.

The ride back home gave me time to reflect on the afternoon. It had been a good one. The faded, sepia-toned memories in my mind had, for a few hours that day, taken on new life and color and vibrancy. Somehow, I felt reconnected and renewed. Those roads had served to reinforce a link with my past and provide me with a sentimental journey that I needed, perhaps more than I knew. And because of that, it's good to know some of those old roads are still around.

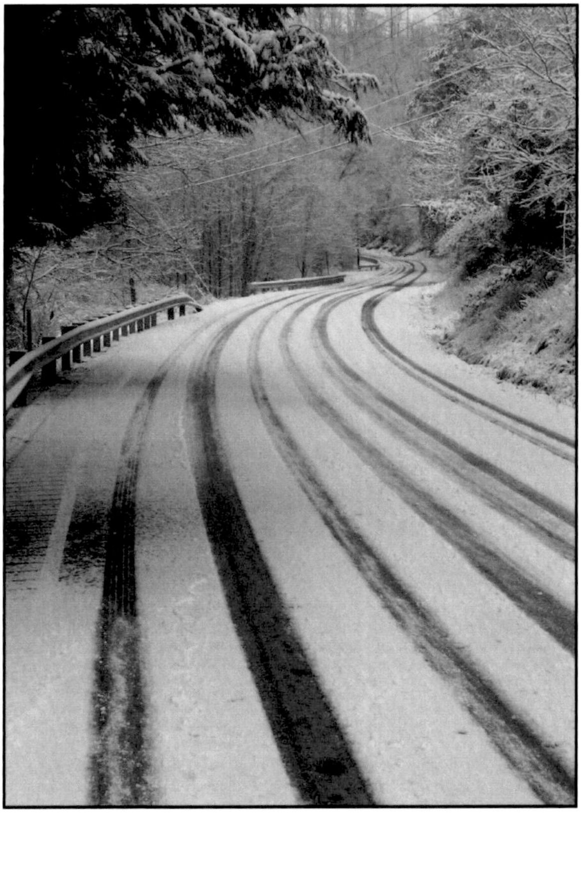

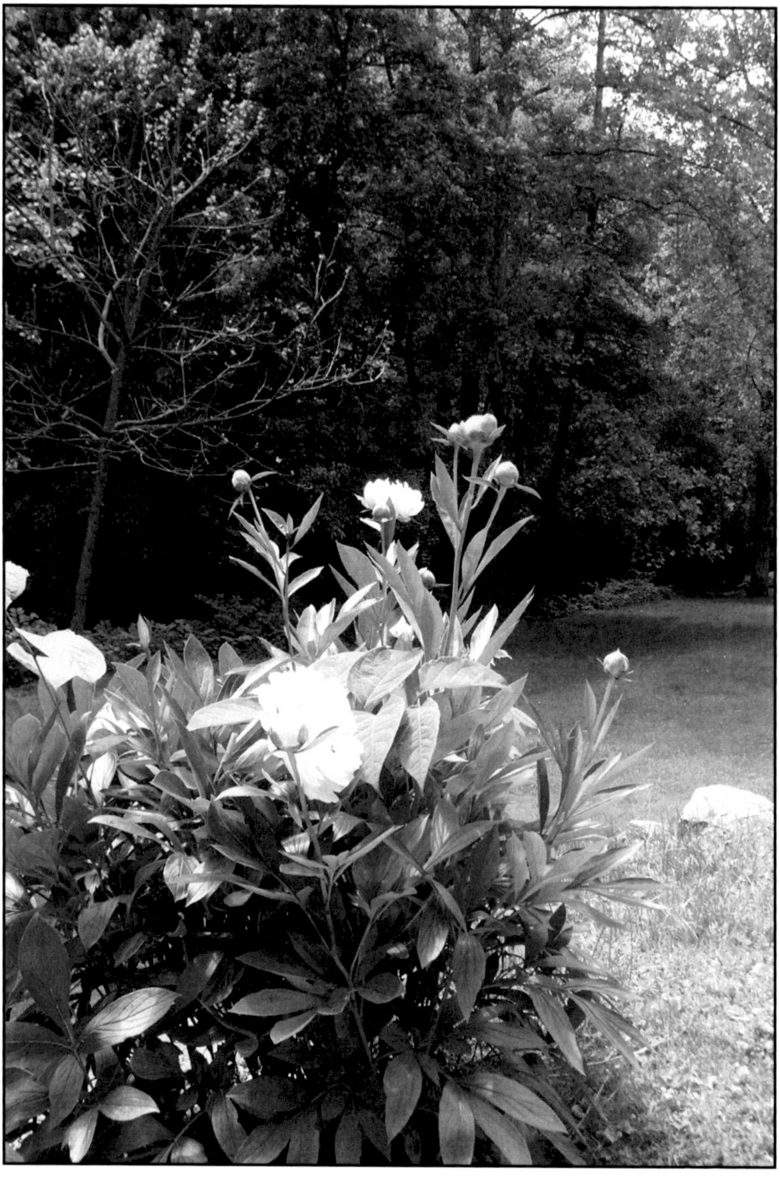

## Like Passin' On Peonies

"Hey, look." I pointed to the other side of the gym. "They're all over yonder."

As we hurried to join our team's other supporters, my friend remarked, "It's sure been a long time since I heard that one."

"Heard what one?"

"Anyone say 'over yonder,' " she replied. Then, smiling, she added, "You have to be of a certain age, you know, to drag that one out of the closet."

Wow, who knew how long that "over yonder" had been hanging around, waiting to jump out and reveal I was "of a certain age?" I had to admit, it had been a long time since I had heard myself or anyone else, for that matter, say 'over yonder.' And, once I started thinking about it, I realized I was missing a whole bunch of words.

The words our great-grandparents, great aunts and

uncles and other older folks used are pretty scarce these days. I miss the mountain phrases and expressions we heard all the time as kids, the ones that seasoned conversations every day. I sometimes wonder if children growing up in this region today will use many of them as they go through life. Do they still hear them?

My great-grandfather used many of those 'old-timey' words. He felt *right pyert* most of the time though, once in a while, he had a *puny spell* and was *ailin'* or worked so hard he was just *tuckered out*. *Nary* a day went by that he didn't walk to the post office, often making a purchase at the country store nearby. He always brought that purchase home in a *poke*. He claimed to be *plumb full* when he ate a lot and about *foundered* on chicken and dumplings.

He *pondered* on things, *aimed* to do certain things, *reckoned* about other things and *took a gander at* things he thought were interesting. He looked for *mare's tails* in the sky that indicated rain and if it came a hard rain, he deemed it a *gulley-washer*. If anything was out of line or not square he said it was *sigogglin*. And he had lived long enough to know sometimes other people can be *a little bit addled* or *just plain quare*.

Papaw was a widower and lived with his daughter, my grandmother. She was up *ginnin' about* early. She never went to town to buy groceries but did go to *trade* and between what she bought and what they raised, she cooked up a lot of *vittles*. If it was *air-ish* out, she grabbed a sweater or coat, knowing if it warmed up, she could always *get shed of it*. When exasperated by some circumstance, she would exclaim, "*Aay, law, children*!" Or, if particularly struck by a new revelation, she'd declare, "*Well, upon my word and honor!*" or "*Why, I never saw the beat!*"

It will be sad if those mountain idioms, words packed up and carted off to '*these parts*' by our forefathers long ago, fall by the wayside as we rush headlong into the future. I don't want to see them fade into the distance, become used less and less, until no one remembers them at all.

Maybe their preservation can be kind of like passin' on peonies. Every spring I look forward to those beautiful old peonies that have been in my family now for generations. As soon as we had a piece of ground to call our own, here they came in a bucket of dirt from Letcher County. My mother, like women in the family before her, dug up some of those peonies and passed them on to the next generation. I have done the same. Just like passin' on peonies, we can make sure we pass on to the next generation the beautiful words that have colored and flavored our language here in the mountains for so many years.

Perhaps, if children growing up here today are to hear those words and someday sprinkle them around as *they* talk, we'd better keep on using them ourselves. And so what if doing that shows I've been around a while? I guess it just means I'm old enough to value their unique qualities and the linguistic history and heritage they represent. Old enough to know some things are worth hanging on to. Even things like words.

Who knows? One of these days I might hear one of my grandchildren say, "Where's my jacket? It's air-ish out." By then, I surely will be "of a certain age." I reckon it will do my old heart good.

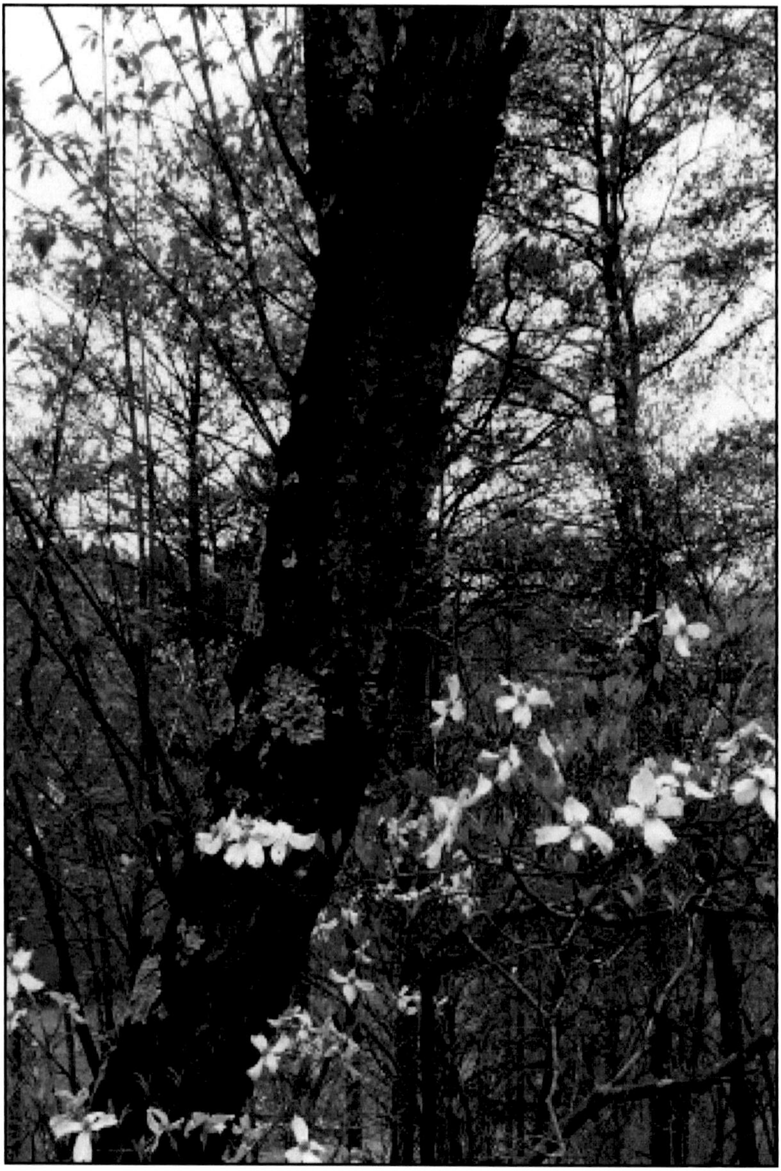

# Appalachian Parade

I've always been curious about how folks ended up settling in the Appalachian region of Kentucky. Many families share a common history, a history taught to schoolchildren all across this region. Their ancestors might have been some of the Revolutionary soldiers who were awarded tracts of steep, mountainside bounty land. Or maybe they were some of the Ulster Scots who set out to tame this jungle-like region and stake a claim in it for themselves. They could have been some of the English folk from over in Virginia who felt a tad stifled and set out looking for a freer kind of life. Or maybe they were just plain outlaws, looking for a place to hide.

They all faced some formidable obstacles. Massive trees, thick undergrowth, wild animals, rugged terrain. Somehow, in spite of it all, they pushed their way through and built a new life for themselves in a new place.

I can't help but be curious about the rest of the story, though. What made them stay? What caused them to put down roots here in the eastern part of Kentucky rather than press on to the fertile farmlands that, all things considered, weren't that far ahead?

I wonder about things like that. Did someone get sick, did a wagon break down, did they really intend to stay 'just a spell' before heading on? Or, as some have speculated, was there something else, especially for those of Scottish descent like the Stewarts in my family, that led them to linger in these mountains? To those whose forebears might have hailed from the coves of Scotland's highlands, did it somehow just look like 'home?'

The romantic, impractical side of me likes to think there was something about springtime in this place that captured their attention. I can't imagine anywhere I'd rather be at that time of year. Though the plants and trees which come to life here today in spring may include varieties they didn't have then, maybe, like me, they still witnessed enough to believe there was no place they would rather be.

Early April is a wonderful time for taking to the hills. When you walk up into the mountains, if you stand very still, you can almost hear it - the early, faint strains of nature's song of regeneration. You can feel it in a fresh gentleness in the air, a stirring, a quiet sense of expectancy and hope that seeps up through the ground and right on through the soles of your shoes. Something is about to happen.

There are fickle moments and starts and stops. The 'little winters' of dogwood, redbud and blackberry, ill-tempered cold snaps or strings of rainy days, make their appearances. Well-known to native sons and daughters, one by one those spells of unwelcome weather march resolutely along. With their damp and cold, they steal away the sun's new-found warmth and send us rummaging back through closets for coats and sweaters again. Persistently week by week, however, that faint chorus builds in intensity until, at last, the mountains around us resonate with the hallelujah of another spring.

We have front row seats for this parade of rebirth, choreographed in slow step, as if the Creator knew we couldn't take it in all at once. Willows draped in spring green. Riotous bursts of forsythia. Ferns unfolding. Splashes of waterfalls gleaming in the sunlight. Redbud blossoms peeking through morning fog. Quince and crabapple and lilac. Wildflowers raising sleepy heads. Hills and hollows laced with flowering dogwood. I could never take it in all at once.

One of the final entries in the parade of spring here in the mountains are the grand old black walnut trees. Well into May, they stand bare in contrast to the other trees around them already dressed in spring finery. One almost feels sorry for them.

No need to. They're only waiting, biding their time in order to practically steal the show with all their glory a few weeks later. An older Letcher County gentleman once told me his mother always cautioned him and his brothers and sisters that they absolutely could not go barefoot until the black walnut trees had leafed out. Then they finally got to shed their shoes and revel in the freedom of another Appalachian spring in the mountains of Kentucky.

So, I can't help but wonder. Could springtime

have played a small part in those older generations settling here? Maybe. More than likely, though, as in many instances in life, their decisions were due to a combination of circumstances, a jumble of things falling together with no rhyme or reason. It doesn't really matter. I'm just glad my clan of Stewarts stayed so that one day I, too, could know the pure delight of spring waterfalls glistening in the sunlight and redbud blossoms peeking through an April morning fog.

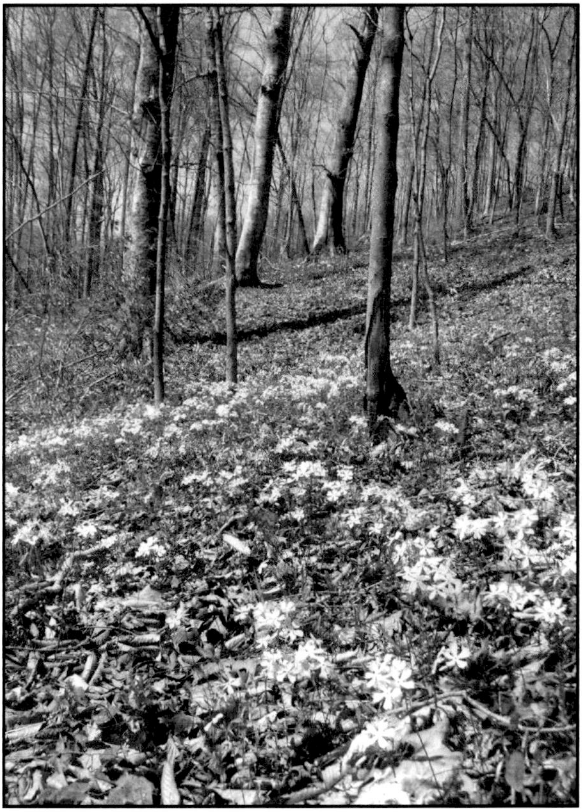

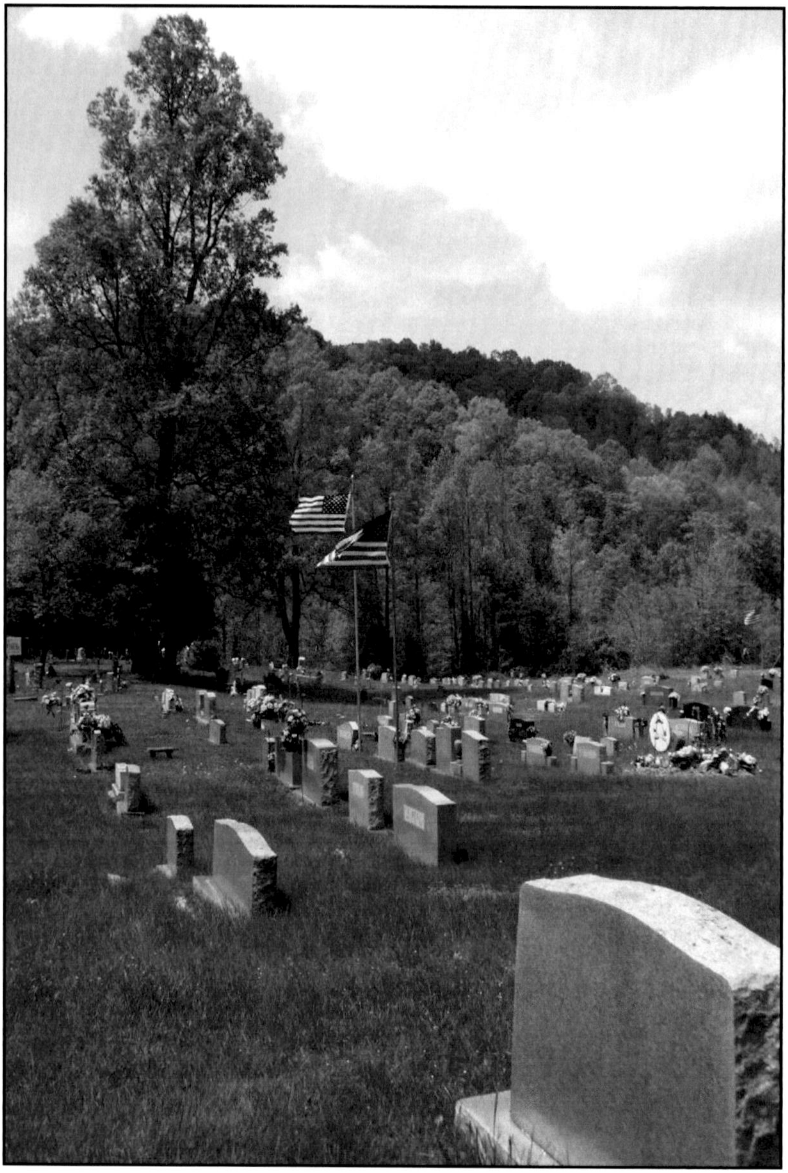

## *Delayed Meeting*

No one writes letters anymore. Not really. The latest letter I received, aside from junk mail and bills, was from a friend well into her eighties, a longstanding member of the generation acquainted with putting pen to paper.

Today, the practice of letter writing seems quaint and old fashioned like southern ladies carrying handkerchiefs and parasols. Cell phones have practically become appendages and enable us to stay in touch with friends and loved ones across the country. Even as we now routinely send e-mail, faxes, leave voicemail and send texts, more communication marvels no doubt lie just around the corner.

However, it was through a regular, honest-to-goodness letter that I met someone not long ago. It was an old letter, mailed and received before I was even born. The person I met was my grandmother.

I always wished I could have known her but my maternal grandmother died tragically when my mother was just a young girl. I often wondered what she was like. Did she laugh a lot? What was her favorite color? What was it like raising her family back then? I never got those questions answered, but I did learn a few things along the way.

Before being employed in other jobs, her husband was a coal miner and early on, like many here in the mountains, they lived in the coal camps. She bore nine children. Two babies died when just a few months old and she lost another child years later, when her oldest son was killed during World War II.

I'd seen a couple of old photographs of my grandmother but, back in those days, cameras weren't part of everyday life for most Appalachian families, especially those of modest means, so pictures were few. Once in a great while, as I grew up, I asked about her but I could sense the pain of her loss was still profound, so I didn't ask a lot. It was easy to see my mother had loved her deeply so I concluded she must have been a pretty wonderful lady.

While visiting an elderly aunt who became sort of the 'family archivist', we looked through old pictures as we had done on many other occasions through the years. She pointed out and named relatives gone long before my time, men, women and children gathered on the steps of simple mountain homes. I studied the faces of the young women who, alongside their husbands, stood with children in their arms or at their feet. They returned my gaze with wistful, shy smiles and eyes that told of the hard work that, no doubt, filled many hours of their days.

That day, after a time sifting through those photographs, my aunt's hand reached for something unfamiliar. She gave a faded envelope to me and asked, "Have you ever seen this?"

I removed an old yellowed letter with the letterhead of Company B, 387th Military Police Battalion, dated March 28, 1945 and began to read. "Dear Mrs. Mullins, Your son, Glenn Mullins, died in the line of duty on the morning of February..." I realized it was the letter notifying the family my uncle had been killed as U.S. troops fought in France.

I thought of my grandmother receiving that news. Who had been with her? How was the letter brought to her? Was she at home when she read those words? I marveled that the same hands that had carried water from the well, made cornbread, braided hair and mended clothes had once held the very letter that was now in my own hands.

And in the crazy way thoughts from out of nowhere sometimes come to mind, I also thought of my mother's finger. To this day, one of her fingers bears a small, odd, bluish-gray discoloration. "Why is your finger like that?" I asked when I was young.

She explained that, as a child, she had cut her finger on some broken glass and it bled profusely. In their home there was not much of anything with which to stop the bleeding, and her mother, acting quickly, employed the old mountain remedy of using soot to seal the wound. These many years later, my mother bears on her finger a tangible memory of the care of the woman she lost so early in life, the woman whose letter I held.

And suddenly, in an instant, I did know my grandmother. As a mother with four children of my own, my heart ached for the anguish she must have felt when she read that letter.

"You have the deepest sympathy of the officers and men in this organization in your bereavement. He was held in high regard by all members of the command. He was a splendid soldier and an outstanding character. His loss is deeply felt by his many friends." Kind words from his commanding officer, cushioning the blow as best he could with praise for her son.

Three good buddies, all from the same southeastern Kentucky community, had enlisted together, my aunt related as I read some of the lines again. Something sort of clicked in my mind. Her statement reminded me of... of what? I closed my eyes a minute. What was it? Then I remembered. It was an article I once read which included General Patton's comments in March, 1944 to men who would serve in his Third Army. Patton had told them to look to their right and then look to their left. After they did so, he went on to remark, "One of you won't be around at the end of the war."

My uncle was the one of the three that did not return to the mountains and creeks of southeastern Kentucky where he loved to hunt and fish. Patton's words were tough and tragically prophetic for so many men. Fine men, exemplary soldiers from all across these mountains. Truck drivers that became tank drivers. Students that became radiomen. Fathers that became platoon leaders. Brothers that became bomber pilots and tail-gunners. So many did not return.

I wiped my eyes and refolded the letter. "No, I had never seen that before," I said. I had never seen my grandmother before that day, either, not in such a real and profound way. And in my heart I felt that I had met her, finally met her, after all those years.

There are mountainside cemeteries all over this region like the little one in Jenkins where my uncle's body was laid to rest. As I witness our country's flag flying proudly above so many of those gravesites, I am ever mindful there were countless other letters just like the one my grandmother received. And countless other brave mountain women who, from these hills of Appalachia, have given to this country some of its very best soldiers.

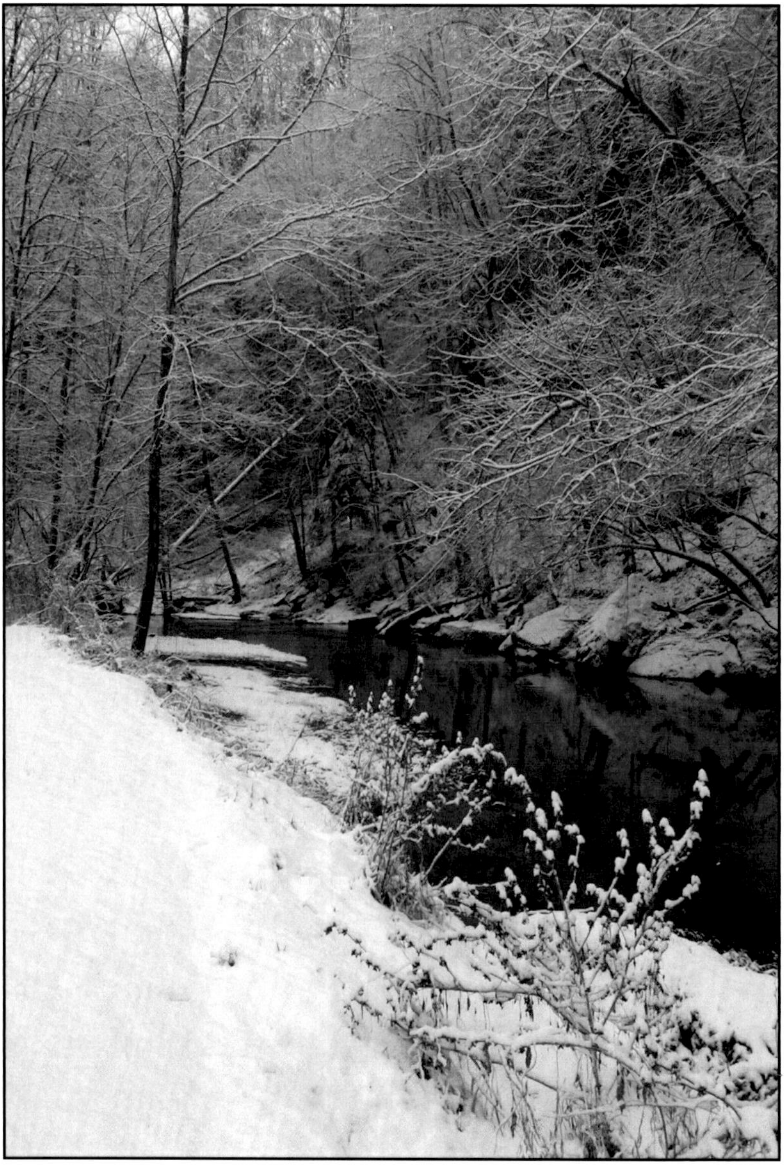

## Just January

Every time I'm at a salad bar and pile several slices of green peppers on my plate, I think about how far I've come. There was a time in my life when I wouldn't have touched a piece of raw green pepper with a ten foot pole. If they were cooked, that was a different story. When simmered in chili, fancied up as stuffed peppers or sautéed and added to other dishes, I liked them very much. But that was the only way I liked them.

I laugh about that now because raw green peppers (and red ones and yellow ones) are among some of my favorite foods. Some things just have to grow on you. That's sort of the way it was with January here in the mountains of Kentucky. It had to grow on me.

When I was much younger, I didn't particularly care for January. I had reasons. I thought the mountains around us, stripped of their beautiful color and foliage at that time of year, were so plain and unattractive. Almost ugly, really. And sometimes, in January, it seems like these old mountains just pull the clouds way down and hang them from the trees. There are stretches of gray, dreary days without a speck of blue in the sky and freezing cold temperatures. Time crawls by at a snail's pace and all we can do is buckle down and wait it out. In my mind, it was always just January, a time to be endured and tolerated until something better came along. Like spring.

Thankfully, the passage of time allows tastes to change and opportunities to see things differently. I like January now. I never thought I'd say it, but I actually look forward to seeing the mountains in the dead of winter and the month of January pretty much qualifies as that. With the busyness of Thanksgiving and Christmas left behind, in the relative quiet of those winter days, all sorts of things suddenly appear. You are able to notice things that, during the rest of the year, just kind of take a backseat.

One of the things I like best about January is that the bare bones of the mountain land, the slopes and shadows, the curves and crinkles, are all revealed. Every leafless tree becomes a sculpture in its own right; each evergreen a lesson in symmetry and balance. Outcroppings of rocks, hidden hollows, streams and trails, fallen trees, countless things covered in other months are unveiled and accessible, at least with our eyes.

And, contrary to what I used to think, there are colors to enjoy at that time of year after all. Copper leaves piled under trees on the mountainsides shine in the afternoon sun like heaps of pennies. Twigs and branches reveal shades of burgundy, russet and gold and sometimes offer glimpses of bright, red berries or left-behind birds' nests. Noble stands of pine and hemlock, their greenery vivid in contrast to their stark companions, bask in freshly-gained attention. The white bark of tall sycamores gleams against topaz skies. Even the pea-green moss fastened to rocks and cliffs seems more vibrant against the muted backdrop of the winter woods.

The month of January can bring snow that transforms the mountains into a minimalist world of white on white, a hushed place where nature rests in quiet repose under its chilly blanket. Ice frosts the creeks in silver and hangs glistening from banks and ledges. Crystal branches sparkle in mid-day sun and cardinals, perched on the ends, seem like scarlet exclamation points.

In the pale light of early evening, smoke curls up from chimneys in the valleys. Pink and purple sunsets, smudged across the horizon like strokes of colored chalk, glow through bare trees on the ridges. Then, finally, a shawl of darkness covers the shoulders of the mountains and folds down into the hollows.

Somehow, it's not just January anymore. I have found that in that quiet, unassuming month there is, indeed, much beauty here. More importantly, I have learned that, sometimes in life, it is not a matter of a lack of beauty for us to see, no matter where we find ourselves. Rather, we often miss it because we fail to look in those unlikely and unexpected places. And I have learned that what was once 'just January,' is really just fine.

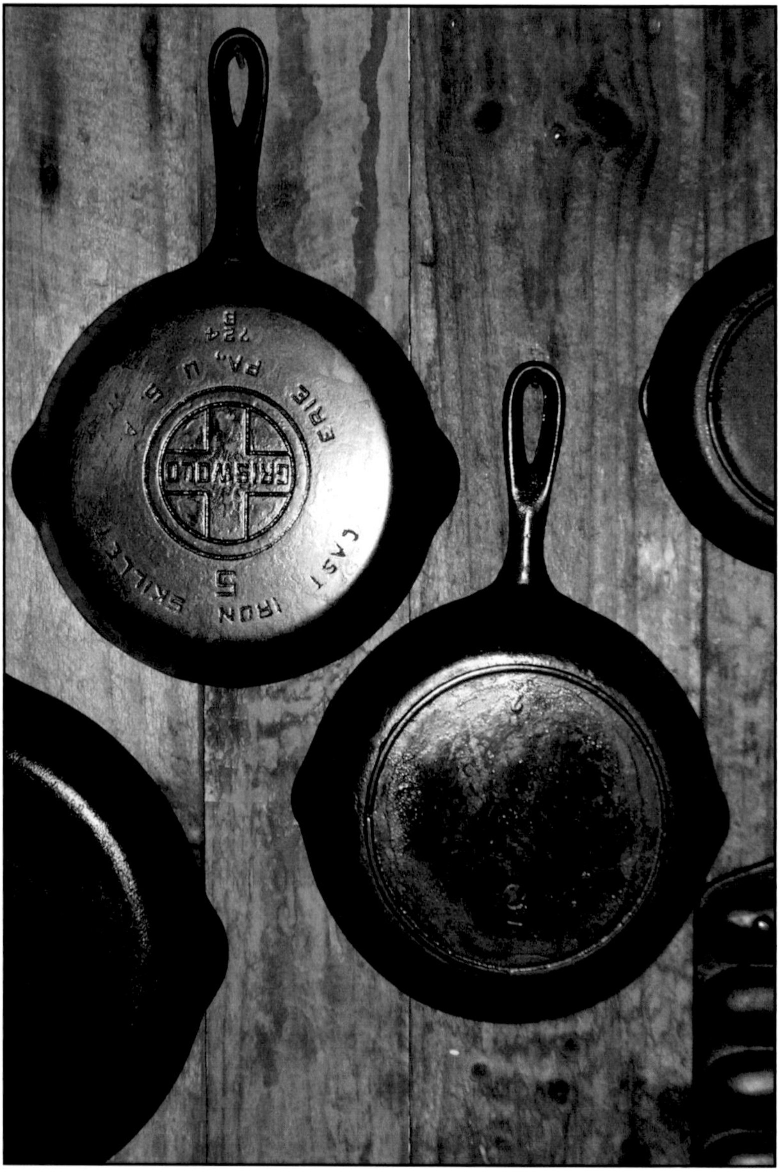
GRISWOLD
ERIE
CAST IRON SKILLET
5

## *Pumping Iron*

Anyone can tell you some awfully good cooks have been raised in these mountains, women who've carried on the tradition of cooking hearty, delicious Appalachian fare for their families. They have been nothing less than some of the 'cookin'est' women on the face of the earth. You couldn't sit five minutes in the homes of Marie Howard or Chloe Pennington, two of the finest cooks Bledsoe, in Harlan County, ever saw, without a plate of tasty home-cooked food appearing in front of you. Over on 16 Mile Creek in Perry County, Stella Pollard's rolled and cut gingerbread cakes melted in your mouth and left a warm, sweet memory of ginger and brown sugar behind. And just up the road a piece, on Lost Creek, Omeda Campbell has, in her lifetime, made some of the finest chicken and dumplings ever tasted.

Those women and others like them, fixed soup

beans and corn bread, shucky beans, biscuits, stack cakes, fresh-cooked beans, and poke sallet. They turned out huge platters of fried chicken, filled big ol' crocks with sauerkraut, baked blackberry cobblers and enough gingerbread to build a bridge over the Kentucky River. And they did a lot of that cooking in old-fashioned cast iron skillets.

I keep coming back to the iron skillets I own though, at times, when trying some newfangled non-stick product, they've hung idly by. One of those skillets was Granny's. She fried chicken, bacon, sausage and ham in it. Made gravy and baked cornbread. Fried eggs and green tomatoes and apples. Under her watchful eye, those apples transformed from crisp, uniform slices into soft morsels that glistened with sweetness against the black of the skillet.

The gravy Granny made for breakfast was flavored with the mixture of flour and sausage drippings she stirred for what seemed like forever. She stood at the stove, her old wooden spoon circling and circling the skillet until its contents browned to the color of caramel and popped with a startled sizzle when she added the milk for the gravy. Our plates were soon mounded with gravy-smothered biscuits, fried apples and pieces of ham or sausage. Eggs, too.

You don't see many ads for plain old cast iron cookware but you'd have to search long and hard for something as durable and versatile. Bits of iron don't begin to flake off after many uses and scratches rarely develop from using the 'wrong utensils.' Over time, should foods begin to stick to their surfaces, you can do what Granny did to re-season hers. She put them in a little fire she built out back. They came out looking ashy and awful but after a good washing and greasing, she'd pronounce them 'slick as a ribbon' and get back to cooking again.

And did I mention their versatility? One long ago day, I returned from an afternoon of shopping, unloaded the car and settled my pre-schoolers down in the kitchen with a snack. In the relative quiet, I heard odd noises in the basement like someone rummaging through things, and then…footsteps. Evidently, we'd come home to an intruder in our house.

My heart raced as I looked around for something to use for a weapon in case the thief came through the basement door and into the kitchen. My eyes fell on Granny's old Griswold skillet, hanging on the kitchen wall. I grabbed it by the handle, with an absurd vision of Granny Clampett brandishing one at her nephew, Jethro, in my head. There I stood, poised, ready to strike. My heart pounded as the basement door's handle turned and our pint-sized, overly-curious neighbor boy entered the kitchen.

After I sighed in relief and lowered my 'weapon', he and I had a discussion about how you don't enter a neighbor's house when they're not home, even if they're careless enough to leave a basement window open. And just what would I have done, I wondered, had there been a bona-fide thief? I believe I'd have let them have it with Granny's skillet, and I don't think the skillet would have been any the worse for wear. I imagine Granny would have been proud to know her old skillet had come to the rescue.

Like I was saying, those cast iron skillets - you just can't beat them for versatility. That's why, when it comes to cooking, I think I'm going back to 'pumping iron' more often. And while I'm at it, I just might get my arms in shape, too.

*"I had six sisters and two brothers. We farmed and gardened and kept a cow. And we had a big apple orchard. We would dry 'em, sulpher 'em, can 'em, ever which way we could fix 'em."*

Minnie Owsley
Knott County
1916-2011

*"Of course, we had to pick up wood for the stove. We'd get out and pick it up here, there and round-about.."*

Maudie Fugate
Knott County
1929-2013

## Stella Pollard's Gingerbread

Sift together:
7 cups plain flour
2 cups dark brown sugar
1 cup white sugar
1 tablespoon baking powder
1 teaspoon baking soda
1 teaspoon allspice
1 teaspoon cinnamon
2 1/2 tablespoons of ginger
Dash of nutmeg
Dash of cloves

Mix together:
3 eggs, room temperature
3/4 cup lard, room temperature
2 cups buttermilk, room temperature

Mix buttermilk mixture with dry ingredients.
Roll out on a floured towel on board.
Toss until smooth.
Cut into pieces.
Bake on cookie sheets for 20 minutes, then brown.

### Dipping Syrup:
1 box dark brown sugar
1 cup hot water
Stir together brown sugar and hot water.
Dip each cake in brown sugar mixture.

*Stella Pollard*
*Perry County*
*1916-2011*

EXIT 43
West Liberty
Paintsville
Pikeville
LEFT LANE
TO 15
Jackson
Hindman
Whitesburg
RIGHT LANE
SPEED LIMIT 55
SPEED LIMIT 55

## My Corner of Kentucky

Like a lot of people, once in a while I place orders for things or take care of business that involves making calls and answering routine questions. With the telephone to my ear, I recite my usual litany. "Debbie - yes, with an 'i-e.' Hodson. No, not Hudson - it's very close, but it's H-o-d-s-o-n. Mm, hmm. Correct. Yes, that is a post office box. Oh. It's Emmalena, Kentucky. That's all one word. I mean the Emmalena part. Sure. E-m-m-a-l-e-n-a. Right. And the zip code is 41740. Yes. Got it?"

Sometimes, perhaps if the person on the other end is having a good day, they make small talk. They say things like, "Emmalena. That's kind of a funny name."

In some instances I just reply, "It is an interesting name, isn't it?" Then, again, perhaps if I'm having a good day, I elaborate. Sometimes, it goes something like this...

"Yes, it's unusual. It was named for a couple of women in this community back in the late 1800's. Emma was the wife of a local school teacher who had a part in bringing the post office into existence and Orlena was the wife of the first postmaster. Someone got the idea to put those two names together and came up with Emmalena. It's just a little spot but, still, a good number of people live in the community."

"Well, isn't that cute?" often is the response. "What part of Kentucky? Is it near Lexington? There's a lot of horse farms there, right?"

"Yes", I say, "There are a lot of horse farms near Lexington. But we're not really near Lexington. That's more in the central part of the state. We're quite a bit further east in the part of Kentucky that has mountains and not so many horse farms."

"Near Louisville?" they want to know, trying to sound knowledgeable and interested.

"Well, no, Louisville is even further away. Emmalena is in southeastern Kentucky, actually."

I can tell it doesn't register. Aware they have a job to do and other calls to take, I restrain myself from commencing a little geography lesson. But I'd sure like to.

"That's okay," I'd say. "Lexington and Louisville are well known places. Some people aren't familiar with this part of Kentucky. Let's say, if you drew a line down the middle of Kentucky from top to bottom, from up near the Ohio River right on down to the Tennessee border, that line would divide the state in half, pretty much into east and west. Technically speaking, it could be said folks living anywhere to the right of that line, live in eastern Kentucky. But, that wouldn't be the southeastern part of Kentucky."

Knowing the person on the other end might barely be with me, I'd still like to forge ahead with my educational endeavor because, well… just because.

I'd explain, "To get to Emmalena and the area of Kentucky where I live, you have to take highways like the Bert Combs Mountain Parkway or the Hal Rogers Parkway and start driving east. If you keep on driving, you'll probably find US 23 or maybe KY 15 or KY 421."

"You'll see highway signs directing you to cities like Hazard and Harlan or Paintsville, Prestonsburg and Pikeville. As you travel further into the region, you'll come across small towns such as Hyden and Hindman and Whitesburg and Cumberland and Jenkins. The mountains will get taller and the valleys will get tighter, and before long, you'll be so far east you can almost reach out and touch Virginia or maybe West Virginia. That's when you'll be in my corner of Kentucky."

"There's some beautiful country here - creeks and lakes and mountaintop views and old-growth forests full of native plants and herbs and wildflowers."

"There are such nice people, kind-hearted, friendly, good people. And some of the best cooks in the world! Do you like homemade gingerbread and chicken and dumplings and biscuits and gravy and... hello, hello?"

I know I'd likely lose them. Oh, well. I guess I can get a bit too carried away when I'm trying to tell people about this part of Kentucky. I can only hope one day they'll be able to come see it for themselves.

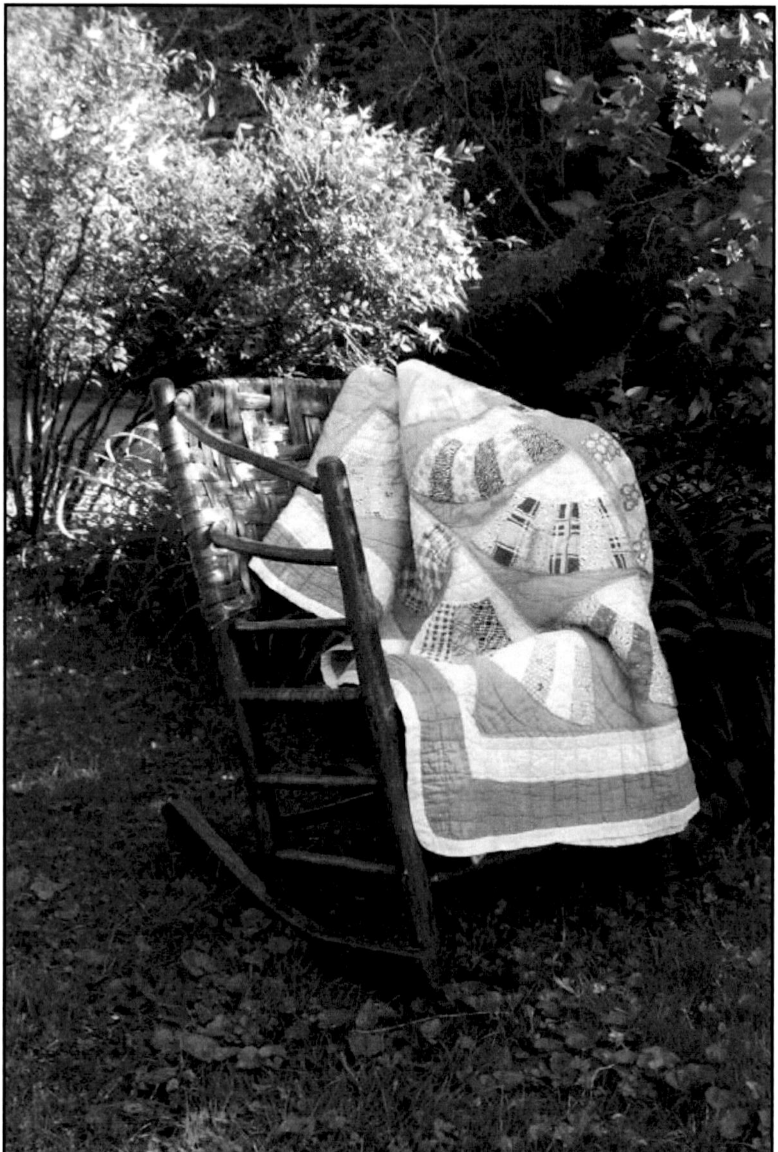

## *Sleeping Under Love*

Appalachian women have quilted for ages. Or close to it. In the earliest days of this area's settlement, however, little time could be devoted to luxuries such as decorative needlework. The women were far too busy spinning and weaving, cooking, carrying water, hoeing corn and raising children to indulge in many other pastimes.

As the nation's textile industry grew, fabric, though still hard to come by, eventually became available to Appalachian women. They quilted not just from necessity, though times were often hard and bed coverings were certainly needed, but, like women today, from a desire to have attractive things for their homes and families. They made do, working with scraps of material, remnants of old clothing, pieces of feed sacks and anything else they could put to use as they set about making their quilts.

I've always been partial to sleeping under quilts. For some reason I never could get enthused about electric blankets or the down comforters many people prefer. A stay with friends a long time ago brought about one of my first encounters with those types of bedding. "Just make yourselves at home," our hostess said as she escorted us to our room. Motioning toward the bed, decked out in an ivory comforter, dust ruffle and matching pillow shams, she added, "I think this down comforter will be enough. We've found it to be very warm, but if you need something more, there's a blanket in the closet. See you in the morning."

The comforter did prove to be all we needed. It was soft and luxurious and, enveloped in a cloud of warmth, we soon dozed off. The next morning, when asked about how well we had slept, I replied, "Oh, we were just fine. That comforter felt wonderful and we were snug as two bugs in a rug." It was true, of course. We did sleep fine, we weren't cold and the comforter didn't slide off the bed in the middle of the night.

I guess I'm just a quilt person, though, and in the fall I find myself dragging mine out from their storage places. A splashy patchwork, made by a friend who lived to be ninety-two, goes on our bed. Granny's leaf quilt is taken to the guest room and others are distributed among the remaining beds.

My favorite, however, is the fan-patterned quilt Granny gave me as a wedding present. It once resided in the big old cedar chest in which she kept the quilts she made over a lifetime. That chest was wide and deep and took up a good amount of room. Various and sundry items such as books and magazines, keys, needles and thread, pocket change and cellophane-wrapped pieces of candy invariably found their way to the top of it.

Once in a while though, on no particular occasion, those things were cleared off and we looked through the contents of the chest. The unique, pleasant aroma of cedar greeted us as we raised the heavy lid and then propped it up on its hinges. And there, waiting patiently, I always thought, for someone to finally open the lid and admire them, rested the quilts.

Quilts with patterns of wedding rings, floral baskets, little Dutch girls, tulips, fans, strawberries, Dresden plates and who knows what else, nestled together in neat stacks. Some, with subdued colors, showed evidence of wear and a few washings while others, obviously unused, remained fresh and bright with fluffy batting. The assortment of colors and patterns amazed me but the careful needlework and the time I knew had been put into each one, amazed me more.

As Granny talked about where she came up with the different patterns and brought out pieces of fabric for me to admire, I engaged in the mental exercise of deciding which quilt I liked best. After dismissing the big, red strawberry-covered quilt and the ones of Dresden plates without too much trouble, it became more of a challenge. The Dutch girls had a certain charm, all standing in cute poses, wearing their odd little shoes. The quilts with wedding ring patterns were pretty and quite interesting, featuring interlocked 'rings' made up of delightfully small pieces. But, no, they really weren't for me.

I might have come close to liking the one with squares of brightly-colored tulips best had it not been for the fan-patterned quilt my eyes kept coming back to. There was something about it. It wasn't one of the new quilts. It was one of those that had been gently used at some point in time and then carefully put away. But, it made me smile. The pieces used for the fans in the quilt were combinations of some of my favorite colors and the sight of such an array of them all together in one place gave me a little jolt of happiness whenever I looked at it.

I remember Granny's face the day she gave that quilt as a present to me. I was young and in love, sporting a sparkle of diamond on my left hand and bustling about with wedding plans. She was older then. The fingers that had once sewn fine, straight stitches had become crooked and misshapen with arthritis, but she still had a twinkle in her eye and a ready smile.

"I thought you might like to have this," she said, holding out something wrapped unceremoniously in brown paper. Glancing up at her with a slightly puzzled look, I tore the plain wrapping away to reveal the fan quilt I'd seen before on our forays into the cedar chest. Bordered with buttery yellow and robin's egg blue, it was filled with fans pieced from solids and prints, pinks and greens, lavenders and yellows, all set on blue squares.

How did Granny know that was the one I would have chosen? I had never told her, at least not with words. Somehow, though, she had just known.

The fan quilt shows its age now in its faded colors and places where the feed sack material used for some pieces has worn thin. I'm reluctant to give it much more wear but keep it over a rocker to grab for naps or reinforcement if it's a two-quilt night.

Granny passed away not long after we were married and while there are pictures to remind us of her and memories of her chicken and dumplings and rhubarb pies, nothing reminds me of her sunny personality and of her love, more than that quilt.

Down comforters are nice, of course, and they make for a restful night's sleep. For all I know, electric blankets may be all right, too, once you get used to them. When you're sleeping under homemade quilts, however, even on the grayest of winter days, you're sleeping under a kaleidoscope of colors. You're snug as a bug in a rug, but best of all, if you're sleeping under a quilt that someone dear to you made, you're sleeping under love.

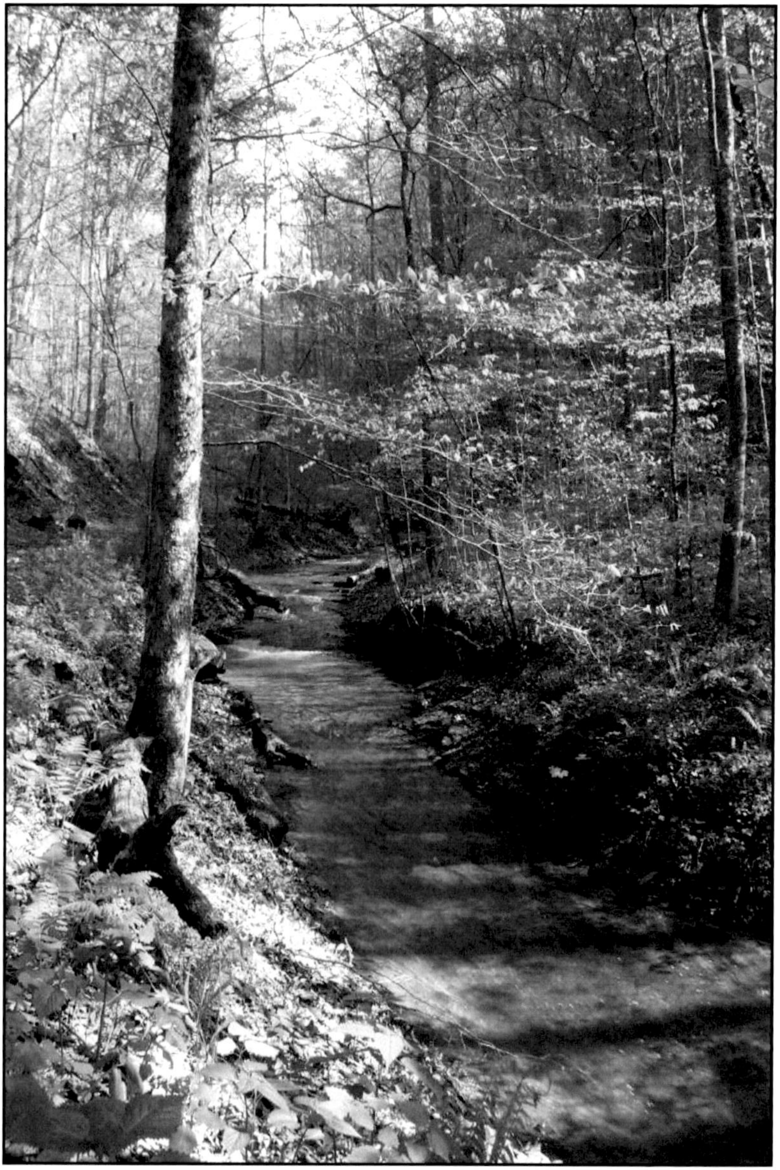

## *Up A Creek*

Dr. Thomas Walker and those with him in the spring of 1750 were among some of the first white men to lay eyes on the rivers, creeks and streams that flow from deep within the mountains of Kentucky. Before heading back to their Virginia homes in July of that year, his account reveals that, among other things, they viewed and named the mighty Cumberland River as it wound through gorges and valleys, erected a log cabin, built a canoe, planted some corn, killed several bears, dealt with a lame horse and faced a humdinger of a storm with torrential rain, downed timber and flooded creeks and streams.

As Walker and his adventurous men forded streams on horseback and foot, it appears they often used the natural characteristics of those waterways in devising names for them. The likes of Cedar Creek, Rocky Creek and Dismal Creek no doubt reflect some aptly chosen.

Troublesome Creek, the little ribbon of water that

flows behind my house, was also appropriately named long ago. Sometimes, it can be troublesome. On some occasions, swollen with rains that tumble down the mountainsides with more burden than it can bear, it rises up and gives us an expanse of waterfront property out back. Fortunately, it lives up to its name infrequently.

Most of the time, old Troublesome just moseys along. From my window I watch the creek transform as seasons change, in turn transporting fallen leaves, chunks of ice, dogwood petals and summer's storm-tossed branches. When rain comes, it churns and muddies and then a day or two later, calms and clears. When rain doesn't come, it slows to a trickle, the rocks in the creek bed stand parched in the sun and minnows and other critters congregate wherever they can find small, remaining pools of water.

The creek rambles on for ninety-nine miles, twisting through the countryside of three counties, before finally joining the North Fork of the Kentucky River. They say Troublesome is just one mile short of qualifying as a river, itself. Though it missed that distinction by just a little, in bygone days the deeper parts of it provided fishin' and swimmin' holes for many mountain children and, over the years, it has kindly supplied water for many a baptizin', too.

In addition to larger creeks like Troublesome, there are countless tiny, shallow streams that run down between the mountains and through the hollows. The thing I like best about these little branches of water is that no special equipment is needed to explore them, providing it's a clean stream, of course. You just need hands and feet that don't mind getting wet. And mine never did.

That's why I always liked to visit a friend who lived off the beaten path, way up at the head of a 'holler.' I was quite envious of her because she had a little creek running right by her house. In fact, one had to drive through portions of it just to get there. I was not quite as fortunate. We lived on the 'main road,' a stretch of highway connecting two small towns, and while more conveniently located, our house was land-locked, with no creek in sight.

Visiting my friend was always an adventure, especially if I got to spend the night. I sat in the back seat as our car wound its way along the hollow's narrow road. After passing numerous houses, a post office and a couple of country stores, the pavement eventually came to an end.

As we traveled the rest of the way up into the 'head of the holler,' the road turned to dirt, with a little gravel scattered here and there for good measure. It was rough and rutted and I bounced along on the seat as the car rocked to and fro. When we finally pulled up in front of my friend's house, I would wave a hasty good-by and scramble out of the car.

After a reasonable amount of time fussing with dolls or playing 'jacks', we often ended up down by the tiny creek. Its water was sometimes reduced to mere puddles, but it was still refreshing, dappled by sunlight that danced its way through the canopy of leaves overhead. Our feet kicked and splashed drops high into the air.

There were turtles and tadpoles, minnows and crawdads. Butterflies and dragonflies darted about and, once in a while, salamanders slid from their damp domains. We explored the creek bank, examining mysterious holes and spider webs, digging into deposits of clay with sticks or bare hands, squishing the gray, slimy stuff through our fingers.

The water-worn rocks lining the creek bed provided smooth, multi-colored specimens for rock collecting. Some were flecked with diamond-like sparkles or had glittery veins in them that led us to believe there just *had* to be gold nearby, if only we could dig far enough into the creek bank to find it.

And we certainly tried. All the while, the summer breeze, laden with fragrances of honeysuckle and roses and freshly-cut grass, carried a bouquet of perfume so sweet we could almost taste it.

Tonight, moonlight touches the ripples and bathes Troublesome Creek in a whitewashed glow. The peaceful, rocking sound of the water washes away the cares of the day almost as easily as it brings back memories of those other days. It seems, like the waters of old Troublesome, the years rhythmically flow into a stream of time that carries us to different places and different seasons in life.

I am certainly not the young girl I used to be, reaching hands into gray, slimy clay. The wrinkles around my eyes and hands that now look suspiciouly like my grandmother's, attest to that. Yet, I know there's a part of me that will always be fascinated by mountain streams and, every now and then, I find my way to places where I can feel the water tumbling over my feet, cup my hands under tiny waterfalls, and bathe my eyes in the wooded green splendor of moss, ferns and lichens and summer leaves draped overhead.

And, whenever I find myself in one of those wet, wonderful places, I can't help but hope there are children out there somewhere still kicking through the creeks, splashing drops of water high into the air. I hope there are some still catching minnows and crawdads, still examining mysterious holes and spider webs. And, I also hope there are some who will get to savor, if only for a fleeting moment, the fantastical idea that, if they dig far enough into the creek bank, they might - just *might* - find gold.

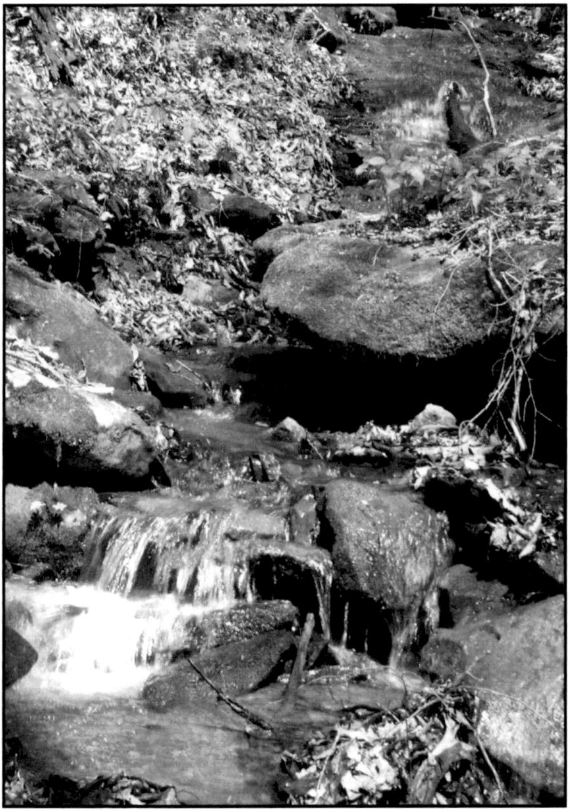